SAN FRANCISCO GIANTS

TORTURE TO RAPTURE

2010 WORLD SERIES CHAMPIONS

San Francisco Chronicle
The Voice of the West
A Hearst Newspaper

Frank J. Vega, Chairman and Publisher

Mark Adkins, President

Gary L. Anderson, Executive Vice President

Ward H. Bushee, Editor and Executive Vice President

Stephen R. Proctor, Managing Editor

Al Saracevic, Sports Editor

Mark Smoyer, Deputy Sports Editor

David Dayton, Assistant Sports Editor

Frank Mina, Assistant Managing Editor/Presentation

Bill Van Niekerken, Project Content Editor

Dan Jung, Project Photo Editor

WRITERS
Bruce Jenkins

Gwen Knapp

Henry Schulman

John Shea

Scott Ostler

PHOTOGRAPHY STAFF
Lacy Atkins

Paul Chinn

Carlos Avila Gonzalez

Liz Hafalia

Lance Iversen

Mike Kepka

Michael Macor

Elly Oxman

Rick Romagosa

John Sebastian Russo

Lea Suzuki

Brant Ward

Russell Yip

Chad Ziemendorf

Peter J. Clark, Publisher   **Molly Voorheis,** Managing Editor   **Nicky Brillowski,** Book and Cover Design

ISBN: 0-9843882-5-7 (PB)
ISBN: 0-9843882-9-5 (HC)

Printed in the United States of America
KCI Sports Publishing   3340 Whiting Avenue, Suite 5   Stevens Point, WI 54481
Phone: 1-800-697-3756   Fax: 715-344-2668
www.kcisports.com

INTRODUCTION

By Al Saracevic,
Chronicle Sports Editor

When the Giants gathered for spring training in late February 2010, great expectations were absent. Most pundits had them picked for second or third place in the National League West, a team with some good young pitchers, but a questionable offense.

Nine months later, a remarkable transformation had taken place. The pitching staff solidified into one of the best in baseball. And a number of midseason acquisitions helped bolster the team's attack.

Nine months later, the Giants had gone from also-rans to world champions.

The story that unfolded between February and November is one of rebirth and reinvention. A tale of perseverance and persistence.

The Giants were rebuilt on the fly by general manager Brian Sabean, who bolstered a foundation of young, homegrown pitching by assembling a lineup consisting largely of journeymen and cast-offs. On the last day of the season, only three starters from Opening Night were in the lineup.

Of course, there was one major anomaly in the plan, and his name was Buster Posey. In many ways, the young catcher's promotion from the minor leagues for the 48th game of the season proved to be the key. This was no veteran addition. Posey was the organization's blue-chip prospect and he became a team leader almost immediately.

The resulting mix of players assembled

Above: Giants manager Bruce Bochy parades the championship trophy for all to see.
Michael Macor | San Francisco Chronicle

by Sabean produced low-scoring, white-knuckle games, often decided by a single run. As announcer Duane Kuiper put it after a particularly painful game in San Diego in April, Giants baseball could be torture for its fans.

And that became the team's unofficial motto: "Giants baseball: Torture." Fans grew to appreciate the team's peculiarities and its penchant for drama. The description grew more and more fitting through a tough stretch drive in which the Giants caught the front-running San Diego Padres, before steamrolling through Atlanta, Philadelphia and Texas in a dominating postseason performance.

INTRODUCTION

And in the end, the torture turned to rapture. Giants fans could justify their suffering by celebrating the team's first championship since the team arrived from New York way back in 1958.

The love affair between the team and its followers was strengthened by the quirky nature of the players. In a city famous for its outspoken citizens and alternative thinking, the Giants' clubhouse at times seemed to be a mirror reflection.

There was Tim Lincecum, the two-time Cy Young Award winner with the long hair and non-conformist attitude. There was Brian Wilson, the eccentric closer who grew a beard, died it jet black and inadvertently created his own catchphrase, "Fear the Beard." And don't forget Aubrey Huff, the offseason pickup who became famous for wearing a red thong under his uniform ... and around the clubhouse. Once again, the fans picked up the team's eccentricities and one could see grown men with lacey thong underwear draped over their baseball hats walking around AT&T Park during the pennant race.

At the center of it all was manager Bruce Bochy, a large man of few words who seemed to make all the right moves late in the season. It was Bochy who had to figure out how to use late-season pickups such as Cody Ross and Mike Fontenot. It was Bochy (along with Sabean) who made the tough choice of leaving millionaire pitcher Barry Zito off the playoff roster. And it was Bochy who stuck by players such as Edgar Renteria. The shortstop ended up hitting two home runs in the World Series and walking away with the MVP trophy.

Through it all, the Giants consistently overcame their naysayers and detractors – many of the same people who had picked them to finish third back in March – by facing up to each successive challenge without flinching. In the playoffs and World Series, a team with supposedly weak bats defeated pitchers such as the Phillies' Roy Halladay and the Rangers' Cliff Lee (twice). The pitching staff stood up to two of the majors' best lineups in Philadelphia and Texas. Not surprisingly, the Giants weren't picked to win either series.

None of the expectations mattered in the end. In Game 5 of the World Series, Lincecum took the mound in Texas and pitched eight innings of stunning baseball, handing the ball to Wilson, his friend and clubhouse neighbor, to get the final three outs.

And Wilson delivered. In their 53rd season in San Francisco, the Giants had won the World Series, four games to one.

The San Francisco Giants have always had great players, from Willie Mays and Willie McCovey to Will Clark and Barry Bonds. But they had not won the World Series while residing on the West Coast.

Back in the Bay Area, the city erupted in celebration, with thousands pouring into the streets in sheer ecstasy. Cars horns honked and strangers hugged.

The torture was over. The rapture had just begun.■

CONTENTS

Balls litter the outfield as players collect them after a drill. *Brant Ward | San Francisco Chronicle*

EYEING DIVISION TITLE, BUT CAN THEY HIT IT?

BY HENRY SCHULMAN

Closer Brian Wilson walked into the clubhouse at Scottsdale Stadium one morning and glanced at a calendar that denoted the scores of every Giants Cactus League game.

He noted the previous day's results and screamed to nobody in particular, "We won yesterday? Oh yeah. That's right. That's what we do."

An 88-74 record in 2009, their first winning record in five seasons, has raised the bar for the Giants in 2010, at least inside the clubhouse, especially among relief pitchers with tattoos and faux-hawk haircuts.

Tim Lincecum authored a metaphor in vogue among the players. Last year, Lincecum said, the Giants opened the door. This year they're going to kick it in.

The holy grail on the other side is a trip to the playoffs for the first time since 2003, a journey that almost all outsiders do not see the Giants taking. Even insiders see it as an uphill climb.

"It's an interesting group," Brian Sabean said of the players he has assembled for his 14th season as general manager. "They know the sense of urgency and I think they know the window of opportunity. It's there for the tak-

ing but they're certainly going to have to earn it. They're going to have to go over two teams, the Dodgers and the Rockies."

Sabean was not discounting the Diamondbacks and Padres, merely noting that the Giants finished third in 2009, Los Angeles and Colorado finished ahead of them and both have the talent to be there again.

A pitching staff that remains the envy of baseball and finished a close second to the Dodgers in ERA last year has the muscle to blow through Lincecum's door.

It seems stronger as Lincecum, Matt Cain and Jonathan Sanchez arrive with another year of experience and with a bullpen that legitimately could run three guys (Dan Runzler, Jeremy Affeldt and Sergio Romo) onto the mound in the ninth inning if something happened to Wilson.

"Sometimes it's just amazing," Wilson said of the starters. "Guys are going seven innings, competing with each other, getting seven 'shutties,' passing the ball over to the next starter. They just feed off each other's energy.

"Pretty loose crowd, too, a lot of great personalities that jell well. Fortunately, they have an amazing amount of talent. That helps. It

Above: New Giants first baseman Aubrey Huff waits for his turn in the batting cage.   *Brant Ward | San Francisco Chronicle*

keeps the pressure off the bullpen, too."

On the other hand, the Giants' offense cannot bust through Lincecum's door. It has to work like termites who bite through it splinter by splinter.

Fans will like Mark DeRosa's approach and

the smoke off Aubrey Huff's bat when he lights into one, but the Giants did not improve enough offensively to challenge the league leaders in runs, on-base percentage and slugging.

That Bengie Molina will hit sixth, not fourth,

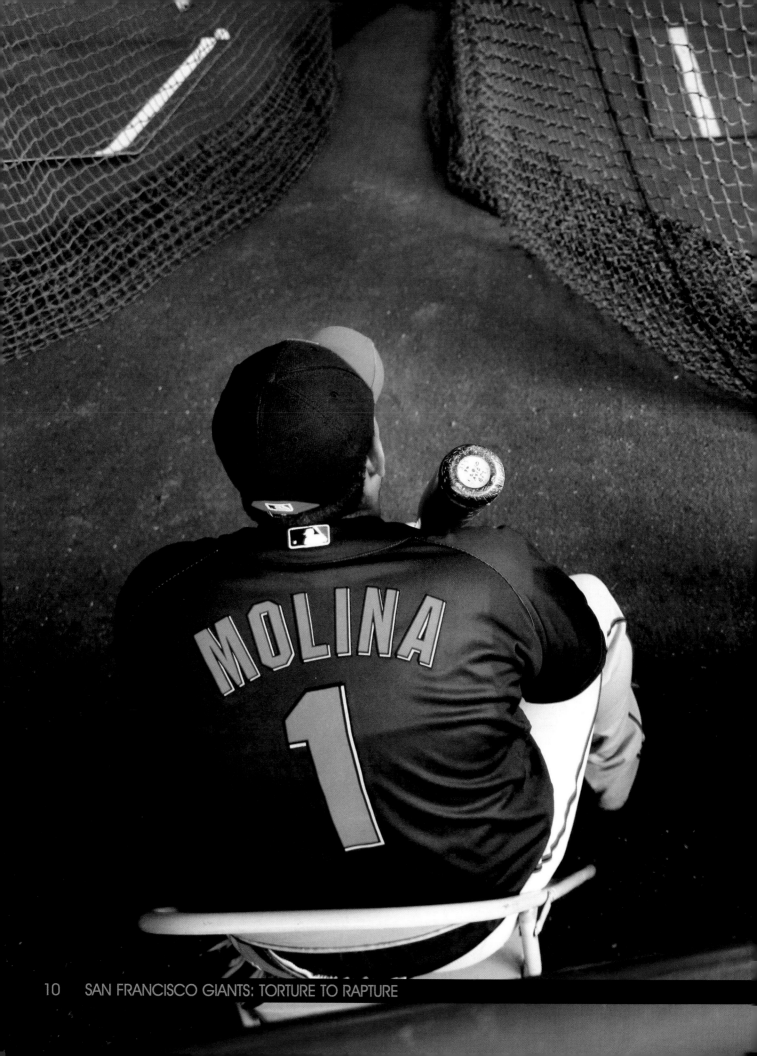

Giants catchers Bengie Molina (left) and Buster Posey (right) talk while waiting for a batting cage opportunity. Many believe Posey will succeed Molina as the Giants regular catcher. *Brant Ward | San Francisco Chronicle*

and Edgar Renteria could be the No. 7 hitter when Freddy Sanchez returns, bespeaks a much deeper lineup, however.

Defense will remain a question until and unless the players answer it in front of wary ticket buyers.

Then comes the C-word, "chemistry," which many fans discount but baseball people do not.

"I think our first asset even beyond our pitching staff is our chemistry," pitcher Barry Zito said. "We added Huff and DeRosa. Not only are they going to add on the field, but they're going to add in a major way in our clubhouse environment. It's so fun to be out there with these guys every day, man. It's such a fun team. Fun translates into relaxation, which translates into getting the most out of your potential."

Will that translate into an NL West title? It will not be easy.

Just before camp broke, managing general partner Bill Neukom called this division the best in the majors, noting the Dodgers and Rockies are perennially strong, and the Diamondbacks and even Padres find ways to frustrate you.

"You look at the other five divisions. I don't think any of them have three or four teams that tough," Neukom said. "It's a terrific division. It's such a difference from four or five years ago, talking about National League Less. We've got to be taken very seriously."∎

Tim Lincecum throws some batting practice. *Brant Ward | San Francisco Chronicle*

LINCECUM STEPS UP, MOWS THEM DOWN

BY HENRY SCHULMAN

It took Roy Oswalt three innings to become Roy Oswalt while Tim Lincecum was Tim Lincecum in the beginning, middle and end. That was the difference in a satisfying opener for the Giants that allowed the two-time Cy Young winner to cross off one of the last remaining nitpicks about him.

Lincecum can pitch – no, dominate – in a big-stage game when his heart might be racing at NASCAR speed. He held the Astros to four singles in seven shutout innings, walked none and struck out seven in a nearly flawless 5-2 San Francisco victory Monday night.

"Just watching him tonight, I got an idea what it's all about," first baseman Aubrey Huff said after seeing Lincecum throw in a regular-season game for the first time. "He knows how to step it up."

That was not true in Lincecum's first Opening Day assignment last year nor when he started the 2009 All-Star Game, both disappointments.

On Monday, it became clear in Inning 1 that Lincecum was going to be The Freak. After Michael Bourn grounded out, Lincecum struck out Kaz Matsui and Hunter Pence on change-ups best described as filth.

Lincecum said an excellent outing against A's minor-leaguers in Phoenix last week gave him the proper frame of mind, even if his heart was tha-thumping a bit.

"It wasn't the kind of hyped-upped-ness where you don't know what's going on," Lincecum said. "Obviously Opening Day can be overwhelming, more exciting than a usual game, but I tried not to let it overwhelm me."

Lincecum not only improved to 34-2 when he gets at least three runs of support, but he also remained unbeaten in four games against Oswalt, among his boyhood idols. Lincecum is 2-0 with a 1.03 ERA, four walks and 28 strike-outs in $26^{1}/_{3}$ innings in games against his diminutive body double.

Lincecum's bed was feathered by a three-run rally against Oswalt in the second. That had to hearten fans who fear another blah offensive year.

Bengie Molina, John Bowker and Juan Uribe each drove in a run after Huff singled in his first Giants at-bat and Mark DeRosa walked on a 3-2 pitch. Once Oswalt left, Edgar Renteria hit a two-out double to cash in Uribe's leadoff single and DeRosa hit an opposite-field homer for his first hit as a Giant.

Above: Tim Lincecum pitches against the Houston Astros on Opening Day. *Chris Graythen | Getty Images*

Mark DeRosa gets a handshake from third base coach Tim Flannery. *Bob Levey | AP Photo*

"That's what we'd like," manager Bruce Bochy said. "It makes life a lot easier when you score early and put crooked numbers up there."

Aside from the superb pitching and timely hitting, the Giants also played well afield in ruining Brad Mills' debut as Houston manager and improving to 7-0 in season openers in Houston.

In his first game as the regular right fielder, Bowker made a stellar running catch in the claustrophobic right-field corner for an out on J.R. Towles. Aaron Rowand went 0-for-5 but motored to the farthest reaches of deep center to rob new Astro Pedro Feliz of extra bases. Pablo Sandoval made a nifty running catch in short left with his back to the plate to retire Geoff Blum.

The Giants' biggest misstep, besides a two-run rally against Brandon Medders in the ninth that necessitated a Brian Wilson save, was Sergio Romo thinking his eighth-inning strikeout of Bourn was the third out when it was the second. He started hopping off the field.

"I was just excited, " Romo said, "caught in the moment on my first Opening Day." ∎

The Giants watch as the jets fly over AT&T Park during opening day ceremonies at the home opener. *Lacy Atkins | San Francisco Chronicle*

OPENING WITH A BANG

BY HENRY SCHULMAN

In brute-force impact, Aaron Rowand's belly-first slide was the TNT equivalent of his nose-first meeting with the center-field fence in Philadelphia years ago.

"Violent," manager Bruce Bochy said.

"Fitting," reliever Sergio Romo called it. "Fitting for that type of game, fitting that he goes head-first into first base and we're now 4-0."

Indeed, the majors' only undefeated team remained so with a 5-4, 13-inning victory over Atlanta in a home opener Friday that will be remembered for two deafening cymbal crashes.

The first was Edgar Renteria's two-run homer with one out in the ninth, on a hanging slider from Billy Wagner, that tied the game 4-4 and actually prompted the new Atlanta closer to say, "He's not hitting .700 for no reason."

The second was Rowand's slide on his two-out infield hit in the 13th that scored Juan Uribe from third to end a 4-hour, 1-minute fight of attrition – Bochy used his entire bench and bullpen – and the longest home opener by innings in San Francisco history.

"Great team win," said Bochy, who would have had Barry Zito throw next had he needed to replace winner Jeremy Affeldt.

There are no trends this early in a season. The sample size is too small. You look at signs, and a lot of the Giants' are positive.

They went to Houston and swept an inferior team.

They rebounded from a 3-0 deficit to win Friday. Last year, it took the Giants 108 games to win a game when they were trailing by at least three.

They beat a good Braves team despite not playing their best. They hit into two first-pitch double plays against Tim Hudson to erase the only baserunners they had in the first six innings. Giants pitchers walked nine, but the offense did not draw one until Uribe's one-out pass in the 13th, which started the winning rally against Kris Medlen.

Though Uribe had only 10 steals over the last five seasons and 13 innings of wear on his legs, Bochy had him run with Rowand up and two outs. Rowand swung at the 0-1 pitch and hit catcher Brian McCann in the chest with his backswing, forcing McCann's throw into center field. That allowed Uribe to take third.

McCann argued for interference, but home-plate umpire Tim Tschida said no, Rowand did nothing wrong. Manager Bobby Cox might have earned his record 154th ejection arguing that call had he not earned it in the top of the inning arguing a strike call.

Medlen's next pitch was the game's last. Rowand grounded one deep into the hole at short. Yunel Escobar gloved it and heaved a

Above: The Giants congratulate Aaron Rowand, who batted in the winning run in the bottom of the 13th inning of the home opener.
Lacy Atkins | San Francisco Chronicle

high throw to first. Rowand would have beaten it standing up but took no chances, and thus his hard belly slide.

"I had no idea how close it was," Rowand said. "I had no idea where the ball was. I knew he went deep into the hole. As soon as I saw him glove it, I put my head down. I still don't know how close it was."

It was close enough that any little contribution helped. Dan Runzler walked home a run in the eighth to give the Braves a 4-2 lead but retired the next two hitters with the bags full to keep it close. Eugenio Velez opened the ninth with a double against Wagner that made Renteria's homer a tying one.

And so on.

"We're just trying to keep things rolling," Rowand said. "Everybody's having fun, and 4-0 is not too bad." ■

CLOSE, BUT NO BLOWN SAVÉ

BY JOHN SHEA

When they crossed paths in the congratulatory high-five line after the Giants' 2-1 victory over the Astros on Saturday, Brian Wilson had a couple of playful questions for Tim Lincecum:

"Why does it always have to be in your starts? Can you give me a bigger lead maybe?"

Wilson was referring to the ninth-inning zaniness he got himself into – and out of – after relieving Lincecum, who pitched eight innings and was hoping the bullpen would maintain his lead for the first time in four starts.

In an outing as weird as it was memorable, Wilson went from having little control to pinpoint control in a matter of moments. He walked two batters, and half of his first 24 pitches were balls. The result: bases loaded, two outs, Kaz Matsui up.

That's when Wilson machined up. Little did he know the .154-hitter would be such a prolonged challenge.

A 15-pitch at-bat ensued. Fourteen fastballs. Twelve strikes. Nine foul balls - five in a row before Matsui finally flied to left field to end the at-bat, inning and game. At last, Lincecum got his fifth win, Wilson his eighth save.

"After a while, it was kind of comical," Wilson said. "How long of an at-bat was it? Felt like a half-hour. So many things going on in my head. I just had to step off and laugh

and look in the dugout – 'What are they thinking right now?'"

Well, Timmy, what were you thinking?

"I didn't feel too nervous," he said. "Wilson was pumping strikes to Matsui. So it was just a matter of whether Matsui was going to put it in play or miss it."

Wilson mixed in one slider on a 2-2 count. Sure enough, Matsui foul-tipped it, and it was too hot to handle for catcher Bengie Molina. So the at-bat resumed. Wilson kept throwing fastballs in the high 90s, and Matsui refused to strike out. One pitch out of the zone would have meant a blown save for Wilson, another no-decision for Lincecum and a faster heart beat for manager Bruce Bochy.

"He had the nerve to ask me after the game, 'Were you worried?'" Bochy said.

Wilson certainly wasn't worried. He said he learned as a closer that it's wiser to be loose than tight, adding, "Can't think of a better time to have recess."

If Matsui had reached base, Bochy said, Jeremy Affeldt would have replaced Wilson. No need. Wilson got it done, and all he needed was 39 pitches.

"I feel bad for the crowd to have them stand that long," Wilson said. "They're probably thinking, 'Gosh, we'd really like to get out of here. Let's go.'"

The Giants scored both runs in the fourth

Above: San Francisco Giants' Brian Wilson, right, is congratulated by catcher Bengie Molina at the end of a game. *AP Photo | Ben Margot*

inning on Juan Uribe's homer off Roy Oswalt after Molina's two-out single. The Astros' run came in the first on a wild pitch by Lincecum, who walked five and struck out five.

"Today," Lincecum said, "was one of those days where I was battling more than pitching." Wilson did both.■

POSEY'S AN INSTANT HIT

BY HENRY SCHULMAN

The 37,400 fans basked in one of those precious moments in San Francisco when they could rise to their feet, cheer a young hitter just up from the minors and say with conviction, "This could be the one."

Think Will Clark, Matt Williams, Royce Clayton or – man, it's been a long time – Buster Posey, whose first big-league game of 2010 on Saturday night was a success.

Posey's contribution in a 12-1 creaming of Arizona was not some Herculean blast to the Coke bottle in left field, but three silky swings that yielded three scoring singles in four at-bats and his first three career RBIs.

Thus, the 23-year-old already delivered on his first promise, just to do his little part and not try to play savior.

"Great job the kid did," manager Bruce Bochy said. "I'm sure he didn't get much sleep last night, and he goes out there and gets some big hits for us. He swung it well down there in Fresno and carried it into tonight. It was a good debut. We needed it."

Officially, Posey was promoted from Triple-A to play first base and get some at-bats until some injured players return. Unofficially, let's just see management send the 2008 first-round draft pick back to the bushes if he hits like this against all foes, not merely the last-place ones.

In his first big-league at-bat of 2010 and the 18th of his career, Posey accomplished in three pitches what took Pablo Sandoval 152 at-bats this year: a two-out hit with a runner in scoring position. Posey's single to center, on a 1-1 fastball from a generally overmatched Billy Buckner in the first inning, brought home Freddy Sanchez.

Posey also hit the last of four consecutive singles in a three-run fifth against Buckner, the other three by Sandoval, Aubrey Huff (now the left fielder) and Juan Uribe. With the bases full and nobody out in the seventh, Posey singled through the hole against Saul Rivera for his third RBI.

That one impressed Huff, who said, "Bases loaded, nobody out. A lot of guys go out and try to do too much. He just took a nice, easy swing, got his hit and got the line moving."

Once Posey got to first after that third hit, he chuckled when base coach Roberto Kelly said, "It's that easy, huh?"

"It's not," Posey said with a laugh.

Sandoval had three more hits and Uribe and Eli Whiteside homered in support of Jonathan Sanchez, who was forced out after five innings because of pitch count but held the Diamondbacks to two hits, including a Rusty Ryal homer, for his first win since April 26. Sanchez walked four and struck out seven.

Even reliever Denny Bautista and little-used Travis Ishikawa joined the offensive fun with

Above: Buster Posey gives the Giants a lift with six hits and four RBIs in his first series. *Carlos Avila Gonzalez | San Francisco Chronicle*

RBI hits.

In fact, Posey's first question after the Giants' biggest scoring day of the season must have been, "This team doesn't hit?"

Bochy said Posey was promoted now because the Giants were down two position players, Edgar Renteria and Mark DeRosa, and "this was a good opportunity for Buster to get some at-bats up here at first base."

Posey's .349 batting average and .995 OPS (on-base plus slugging percentage) at Fresno might have forced the Giants' hand, too.

Bochy would not commit to Posey being here for the rest of the season, saying his sta-tus will be reassessed once Renteria and DeRosa return.

Bochy had not met with Posey before bat-ting practice to give him the "be yourself" speech, but maybe he did not have to. When Posey was asked how aware he was of the clamor for him, he said, "I can honestly, hon-estly say I've tried my best to focus on Fresno and working each day and staying out of the articles and whatnot. I heard things here and there, but I focused on each game.

"There are a lot of good hitters on this team. I don't feel I have to do a lot of extraor-dinary things to help us get a win."▪

WACKY END TO SKID – S.F. TIPS COLORADO

BY HENRY SCHULMAN

When future fans thumb through the 2010 game log and see that the Giants ended their seven-game losing streak with an 11-8 victory at Coors Field, they surely will say, "There must be a wacky story behind that one," and there was.

The Giants on Saturday night dealt the majors' best pitcher one of the worst beatings of his career, yet he did not lose. San Francisco's $126 million pitcher had a 7-1 lead, yet he did not win.

Despite a seven-run third inning against 14-game winner Ubaldo Jimenez, capped by Travis Ishikawa's first career grand slam, the Giants had to come from behind to win, and manager Bruce Bochy was not in the dugout when the skid finally ended because he had been ejected.

Beggars can't be choosers, right? The Giants will take it and do their best to gain a split of the series this afternoon.

"You can't say enough about the grit they played with," Bochy said of his men. "Anytime you cough up a lead like that, it's disheartening, but they didn't show it. They came right back and retook the lead. There's a lot of fight in this club."

The Giants were down 8-7 when they scored twice in the seventh inning against the Rockies' bullpen. Nate Schierholtz hit a lead-off triple and Andres Torres an RBI single. Freddy Sanchez also singled, and after Torres stole third, he was able to score the go-ahead run on Pablo Sandoval's sacrifice fly to center.

Aubrey Huff, who crazily enough predicted a date with Jimenez might be what this reeling team needed, sealed the win with a two-run homer in the ninth, his 15th on the year and third in the span of nine at-bats.

Also credit Sergio Romo, Jeremy Affeldt and Brian Wilson (save No. 22) for holding the Rockies scoreless over the final three innings, no mean feat the way these teams were lighting up the scoreboard.

Once the Rockies scored seven runs in a row to take the lead, it would have been hard to find a bookie willing to lay odds on a Giants win, but they were desperate.

"After losing so many in a row, we weren't going to roll over and die," Schierholtz said.

This was a big night for Schierholtz and Ishikawa, who had been shoved into the farthest recesses of Bochy's closet. Bochy said Ishikawa has "forced the issue" with his hit-

ting of late.

A Giants offense that had not scored more than three runs in a game during the streak already had that many in the third inning, when Ishikawa faced Jimenez. Aaron Rowand hit a leadoff double, Sanchez drove in a run with a single and Sandoval singled home a run. Juan Uribe and Buster Posey walked to load the bases for Ishikawa, who hit a first-pitch fastball into the Rockies' bullpen.

Ishikawa had not started since May 19. Before the game, bench coach Ron Wotus razzed him by pointing toward first base and saying, "See? That's where you run to when the game starts."

Ishikawa has prospered and coped with his reduced role.

"You guys haven't seen me break anything in the clubhouse yet, so I guess I've done a decent job," said Ishikawa, who will start the series finale today.

Barry Zito let the Rockies creep back into the game. He ultimately left in the sixth inning and watched as Dexter Fowler pooched a two-run single to center off Denny Bautista to tie the game. The Rockies took the lead on a Carlos Gonzalez sacrifice fly, made possible by a "safe" call at first that led to Bochy's ejection.∎

Above: Colorado Rockies starting pither Ubaldo Jimenez, bottom, reacts after giving up a grand slam to San Francisco Giants' Travis Ishikawa. *AP Photo | David Zalubowski*

AUBREY HUFF

FINALLY, A DEFINING MOMENT

BY JOHN SHEA

Aubrey Huff played 10 years in the majors before joining the Giants. Mostly with Tampa Bay (in the awful years) and Baltimore. Always on teams that failed to reach the playoffs.

He collected 1,391 hits in those years. None that he wanted to define his career. He added 165 this season, including a memorable double off San Diego's Mat Latos in the regular-season finale that helped clinch the National League West flag.

Which Huff considered the biggest hit of his career to that point.

So when he was asked if Sunday's single that tied Game 3 of the National League Division Series in the ninth inning was No. 1 on his hit chart, he didn't hesitate with an answer.

"Shut your mouth," he said. "What else would be a bigger hit? Baltimore in mid-July? Off the Rays? Of course it was."

The magnitude of the hit skyrocketed once the 2-2 tie was broken when Freddy Sanchez scored after second baseman Brooks Conrad mishandled Buster Posey's grounder, Conrad's third error of the day. The Giants won 3-2 to take a 2-1 advantage in the Division Series, and Huff's career has a defining moment on which he can hang his cap.

With more to come in the coming days and weeks? That's getting ahead of the story, which is about a 33-year-old first baseman who said he seriously considered retirement in recent years, frustrated with playing on teams going nowhere, constantly getting bullied by bigger and badder teams.

With the Giants, his career and spirits have been revitalized. He was the team's most consistent player through the regular season, hitting .290 and leading the club with 26 homers and 86 RBIs. In fact, he was the only man in Sunday's lineup who played the same position in the Opening Day lineup.

His bat momentarily went cold once the postseason started. He was 1-for-10 with five strikeouts and no balls out of the infield. He snapped out of it in his last two at-bats Sunday. His eighth-inning grounder through the middle didn't lead to a run – he was stranded at second as Juan Uribe and Mike Fontenot struck out – but it made him feel more comfortable at the plate.

Above: Aubrey Huff has a look around during introductions.
Michael Macor | San Franciso Chronicle

In the ninth, the Giants were one strike from losing 2-1, but Freddy Sanchez singled to push Travis Ishikawa to second. Huff admitted to being nervous in the on-deck circle, especially when the Braves were making a pitching change: right-hander Craig Kimbrel out, lefty Mike Dunn in.

Once Huff got in the box, he suddenly had a unique feel about the moment.

"Surprisingly calm. It was weird," Huff said. "I don't know, the baseball gods owe me."

Huff took a first-pitch fastball for a strike and made contact on a slider, lifting the ball to right field. Not a hard liner. Not a soft fly. Huff called it "the longest medium flyball I've ever hit. I didn't

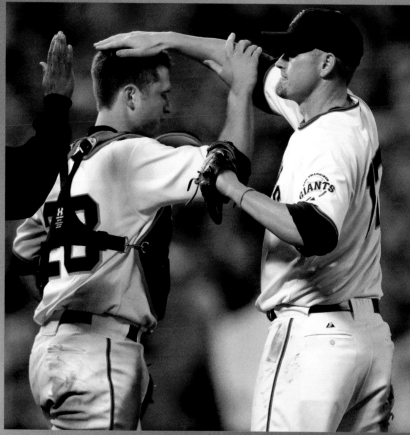

Above: Buster Posey gets a pat on the head from first baseman, Aubrey Huff.
Carlos Avila Gonzalez | San Franciso Chronicle

Below: Aubrey Huff is showered with beer as the Giants celebrate their NL West title.
Chad Ziemendorf | San Franciso Chronicle

think it was ever going to get down." It did. Right in front of Jason Heyward, whose throw home was off-line and failed to catch Ishikawa, who ran for himself because the fast guys the Giants had in September aren't on the playoff roster.

RBI single, Huff.

Followed by an E-4 on Posey's grounder, putting the Giants up 3-2.

Followed by Huff getting to base-ball heaven. Or at least baseball pur-gatory.

"Big hit," manager Bruce Bochy said. "He'd probably tell you it could be one of the biggest hits he's gotten."

Don't go there, Bruce.

Ishikawa was happy for Huff. He's Huff's backup and often replaces him defensively late in games. Ishikawa calls him inspirational, "a joy to have in the clubhouse. He lifts everyone's spirits. I don't think there's a negative thought in his mind. After tough loss-es or big wins, he's always got some-thing positive to say."

On a personal note, Ishikawa added, "I guess I can say I'm very for-tunate in my second or third year to be in my first playoffs. Aubrey's been waiting 10 years. We've talked about it. This is the most fun I've ever had on a baseball field, and I'm glad he's having this experience."

Sanchez can relate. He played most of his career with the Pirates, who haven't had a winning season since the Bonds administration. It was Sanchez who kept the rally alive with his two-out, two-strike single and gave Huff the opportunity of a lifetime.

Sanchez didn't seem as tickled as Huff and wouldn't say his single was the biggest hit of his career. "Not to say we haven't had a lot of big hits in our careers, you know what I mean?" said Sanchez, the 2006 NL batting champ. "But obviously, this is what we play for, the playoffs. It's an unbeliev-able feeling."

Even for a guy limping through the clubhouse. Huff was hurting after this one, having fouled a pitch off his right shin. The physical pain he was feeling was outweighed by the moment he was relishing.

It's about time.∎

Pat Burrell blasts a 2-run homer to left to push the Giants ahead of the Dodgers. *Chad Ziemendorf | San Francisco Chronicle*

LATE-INNING HEROICS PROMPT BURST OF JOY

BY BRUCE JENKINS

Aubrey Huff wore the look of a crazy man, so excited about his friend and his team, he could not contain himself. Each day with the Giants is a treat for Huff, but this was something else, one of those seminal moments against the Dodgers and an unforgettable Saturday afternoon for a sellout crowd at AT&T Park.

Pat Burrell's two-run homer in the eighth inning, a sudden bolt of lightning against Jonathan Broxton, caused one of the wildest regular-season dugout scenes in recent Giants history. Players were shouting, lurching uncontrollably, pounding each other in exultation as the Giants turned a deathly quiet performance into a 2-1 lead. Huff, as one observer noted, "looked like his hair was on fire." Face reddening, veins popping out of his neck, he seemed on the verge of literally bursting with joy.

And here's what Huff found so refreshing: It wasn't about him.

For nine years, Huff had come to believe that baseball was a selfish game. He couldn't hook up with a contender to save his life, so he could only take solace in a home run, a 3-for-4 night, something that might bolster his

career down the line. What Huff has realized this season, and particularly Saturday, is that the finest baseball moments are the residue of teamwork.

Huff has known Burrell since their collegiate days at Miami, and they've stayed close over the years. Both of them came to the Giants with dubious reputations, guys who were portrayed as disruptive influences in the clubhouse and probably not worth the trouble.

Score two massive notches for Brian Sabean. Huff is a legitimate MVP candidate, Burrell officially joined the party with Saturday's game-deciding home run, and the clubhouse could not be more cohesive.

"There are people out there who never played the game, and they just make stuff up," Huff said. "They said I was a bad clubhouse guy when I came here. They said I couldn't play defense. Pat Burrell? He's as good a teammate as you could ever have. Even when he's not playing, he's into the game, giving guys positive feedback. He's a good team guy, man."

Over in another corner of the postgame clubhouse, Andres Torres couldn't get over

Above: San Francisco Giants' Pat Burrell, left, is greeted by Aubrey Huff, right, at home plate after he hit a home run. *Lance Iversen | San Francisco Chronicle*

the atmosphere in the ballpark with the Dodgers in town. "What intensity," he said. "Beat L.A.! You feel like you're in the playoffs right here. The fans get you so fired up to play. It's not about yourself; it's about everybody. The fans are a big part of us."

And Huff? "He looked like a little kid," Torres said, as the team celebrated Burrell's homer. Like a kid whose team had just won it all.

"That's the coolest game I've ever been a part of," Huff said. "To have Pat go deep like that, I felt like a proud papa. I felt like I'd done it. I just started hitting everybody, for no reason (laughter). I probably put some people on the disabled list."

So much is going right for the Giants right now, they laughed at the trading deadline – at least as it involved run production, settling for a pair of relief pitchers (Javier Lopez and Ramon Ramirez) in their Saturday deals. One of the incumbent relievers, Guillermo Mota, revealed that he had joined several teammates in a debate: Who would be the best pickup in a trade, Jose Guillen (the hard-hitting veteran

in Kansas City) or Jose Bautista (a major league-leading 31 homers in Toronto)?

It's a pretty good question, but in the wake of the Giants' surge, said Mota, "I guess we don't need either one of 'em."

In the meantime, a shirtless Jonathan Sanchez walked across the clubhouse floor, flexing his modest biceps and smiling broadly. The deadline has passed, and Sanchez isn't going anywhere. The Giants aren't going to mess with their starting rotation, and assuming Brian Wilson gets over the injury (back spasms) that has kept him out of action the past two games, they're in solid position to make a run for October.

Well after the game, in the glory of late-afternoon sunshine, the field was flooded with fans enjoying a Giants promotion called "Picnic in the Park." There was no sign of blankets, cheese sandwiches or ants, but it was a festival. People were basically just milling around contentedly, basking in the glow of a big victory over the Dodgers. There was no good reason to leave.■

POOR L.A. – NOTHING GOES RIGHT

BY SCOTT OSTLER

It's appalling, the treatment the Giants accorded their guests over the weekend. How many ways can the Dodgers be mistreated and disrespected?

Sunday evening, the visitors from the south were beaten down by ESPN, Deputy Dawg, Lou Seal and Edgar Renteria, not necessarily in that order.

If the three-game series had been a teeter-totter, the Giants would be the mean-spirited fat kid launching the little kid into orbit.

Deputy Dawg? That's Giants manager Bruce Bochy. When Dodgers third baseman Casey Blake came to bat in the second inning, Bochy yelled something from the dugout.

He was telling plate umpire Joe West that Blake was standing too far back in the batter's box. The back line was rubbed out by then, but West asked Blake for his bat, placed it on the ground next to the plate as a measuring stick and told Blake he had to move up a bit. A tiny bit closer to hard-throwing Matt Cain.

Maybe it made no difference, but Blake struck out, the first of his three strikeouts on the day.

Remember how on July 20 at Dodger Stadium, Bochy got Dodgers closer Jonathan Broxton removed from the game by calling the umps' attention to coach Don Mattingly's "second visit" to the mound, when Mattingly turned around briefly and stepped back onto the mound dirt.

Bochy, asked Sunday if it was unusual for a batter to set up too deep, as Blake did, said, deadpan, "It's illegal."

Don't think the Dodgers enjoy being nipped at by Deputy Dawg.

If the players on both teams have a hard time summoning up the crazy intensity of the Dodgers-Giants rivalry that existed 20 and 30 years ago, Bochy is right there, showing them how it's done.

Of even more glaring import Sunday was the 5:10 p.m. starting time, moved back four hours to accommodate the fine folks at ESPN.

When Renteria came to bat in the bottom of the sixth of the scoreless tie, with two outs and two on, the setting sun was hovering just over the grandstand behind home plate.

Dodgers starter Clayton Kershaw had walked Aaron Rowand intentionally to get to Renteria, at least partially because Renteria was 0-for-10 lifetime against Kershaw and had already whiffed once.

Above: Matt Kemp of the Dodgers is tagged by Edgar Renteria in a rundown between first and second base.
John Sebastian Russo | San Francisco Chronicle

Still, as Renteria said, "You don't want to wake up the baby."

The baby smoked a low line drive to left-center. Centerfielder Matt Kemp froze and the ball screamed into the gap, a two-run triple.

"Kemp had no chance at it," Bochy said."As soon as (Renteria) hit it, we knew it was in the gap."

Not so, said Kemp.

"The ball was in the sun and it wouldn't come out," Kemp said. "Definitely, if the sun wasn't like that, I'm catching that."

So Bochy and Kemp will agree to disagree, but Kemp was either sound asleep or blinded, because he never moved.

As for Renteria, this was a high point in his two-season career with the Giants. He's been struggling, 3-for-22 on the homestand before the triple, and has been relegated to half-duty as a starting shortstop, sharing with Juan Uribe.

Sunday, Renteria not only drove in the game's only runs, he made the defensive play of the game, a 360-degree spin and throw-out of Russell Martin in the third inning.

Even mascot Lou Seal got in on the Dodger disrespect. When Seal drove his golf cart around the perimeter of the field after the fifth inning, tossing T-shirts to fans, he drove the cart directly over the Dodgers' bullpen mound. Maybe the Dodgers didn't notice, but I think we all know how Dallas Braden would feel about such a move. He would have had a spike strip ready for Seal the next time.

You talk about hitting a team when it's down. The Dodgers are in the middle of a 10-game stretch against the Padres and Giants, and they are 1-5 so far. Floundering doesn't begin to describe it.

L.A. Times columnist T.J. Simers, who doesn't do subtlety, has taken to referring to the L.A. team in print as the Choking Dogs, and so far Simers has not heard one woof of protest in the clubhouse.

The Dodgers surely felt they nicked the Giants' spirit when they beat the trade deadline by scooping up left fielder/leadoff man Scott Podsednik, whom the Giants had targeted.

When Podsednik led off the game, his batting average flashed on the message board: .182. Actually that was his Dodgers BA; his actual batting average for the season was .307 at the time. Podsednik popped up.

The Dodgers, I tell you, they can't get no respect.■

VICTORY A LONG TIME COMING

BY JOHN SHEA

It took 11 innings. And three hours and 34 minutes. And one of the biggest broken-bat groundouts of the season. And five relievers throwing shutout ball. And a Giants catcher actually stretching a single into a double. And a game-ending single that did in the majors' best bullpen.

The Giants finally proved they needn't keep losing to the Padres.

Juan Uribe singled home Buster Posey for a 3-2 Giants victory Saturday, and suddenly the first-place Padres aren't so invincible. Suddenly, the Giants are thinking about winning a series. Newcomer Jose Guillen will be in the lineup for today's finale, and Tim Lincecum will try to be good ol' Timmy, having shelved his hands-over-the-head windup.

After going 1-8 against the Padres, momentum at last arrived.

"It's a big win," Giants manager Bruce Bochy said. "It gets to the point where you start thinking about it too much. They won a lot of these games, and three or four could've gone the other way, just like today. You've got two good teams scrapping for runs, and it's good to come out on top."

Excuse Posey for knowing little about the Padres' one-sidedness. By the time he arrived from the minors May 29, the Giants were in a 1-7 hole. This series is his first look at the San Diegans, and he's already a difference-maker.

He opened the 11th inning with a grounder up the middle, off second baseman Jerry Hairston Jr.'s glove. As the ball rolled slowly from Hairston, Posey alertly hustled to second, putting him in position to score on Uribe's hit.

"I didn't know he was that fast," said Bochy, perhaps having Bengie Molina flashbacks. "Good hustle on his part. He won the game for us."

Posey slid across the plate, jumped in the air and waved an arm in his most animated moment with the Giants. He was typically even-keeled at his locker afterward, saying of the teams' season series, "It doesn't really matter what happened in the past."

It's hard to overlook, though. Seven of the 10 games were decided by one run. None of the others was decided by more than three. As Aubrey Huff said, "Winning today, we can come out tomorrow a little looser, and maybe we can try to win by a little more than one run."

Above: Sergio Romo celebrates a key out in the extra-inning win over the Padres. *Lance Iversen | San Francisco Chronicle*

Above: San Francisco Giants pitcher Santiago Casilla. *Lance Iversen | San Francisco Chronicle*
Opposite Page: Brian Wilson, left, greets Buster Posey, right, after Posey crossed home plate with the winning run on a Juan Uribe hit in the 11th inning. *Lance Iversen | San Francisco Chronicle*

Lincecum is coming off a rough start against the Cubs, yielding four first-inning runs for the first time in his career, and said he's reverting to his old windup. It seemed his decision, though he said he chatted with his father/mentor, Chris, between starts.

"Just trying to simplify things and get to what I was doing. Not too many moving parts," Lincecum said.

The Giants fell behind 2-0 Saturday with nemesis Mat Latos in control, but recharged Pablo Sandoval homered to open the sev-enth, chasing Latos, who twice beat the Giants 1-0.

The Giants tied it in the eighth when Mike Fontenot singled, advanced to third on Huff's double and scored on Pat Burrell's broken-bat RBI groundout to second, which earned Burrell a big ovation.

Chris Ray, Javier Lopez, Brian Wilson, Sergio Romo and winner Santiago Casilla combined for four shutout innings after Madison Bumgarner gave up two runs on eight hits in seven.■

ROTATION
LOOKS TO SPIN
IN A BETTER DIRECTION

BY HENRY SCHULMAN

If the stark numbers did not appear in black and white, nobody would believe them. Thus far in August, the Giants' rotation has the worst ERA in the National League at 5.20. In the majors, only Cleveland's starters have been worse (5.40).

The Giants are 11-12 this month and leading the National League wild-card standings by half a game with 34 to play. For that, they largely can thank an offense that has scored some runs, including some late heroics at home, and a handful of strong pitching performances at opportune times. But they understand that to go to the playoffs for the first time since 2003, the rotation – around which this team is built – must have a stronger September.

Tonight's game against Arizona at AT&T Park is important, in the standings and symbolically.

Tim Lincecum, enduring the worst month of his career, starts the first of five games that will run through the end of August. The rotation, so battered and bruised during a month that included a 14-game winless stretch for the starters, gets one final turn before September to declare that it will join an improved lineup in a strong push for the postseason.

After an 8-2 loss to the Padres on Aug. 15, Lincecum said, "I can't keep searching. I've got to go out there and pitch."

That is the perfect motto for the starters. They must trust the good stuff they all possess. They know what they can accomplish. The Giants' rotation still has the league's fifth-best ERA for the entire season (3.76) despite the bloated August numbers.

During the 14-game winless drought from Aug. 4 to 18 with a pair of Jonathan Sanchez victories as bookends, the starters were 0-9 with a 5.35 ERA.

There were a few diamonds in the rough. Barry Zito held Atlanta to two runs in seven innings in a 3-2, 11-inning road win on Aug. 6. Madison Bumgarner had the same numbers in that thrilling 3-2 home win against San Diego on Aug. 14, with the rookie getting no decision.

Overall, though, the rotation had only five so-called quality starts (at least six innings, three or fewer runs), two by Matt Cain and one each by Lincecum, Zito and Bumgarner.

Most pitchers go through funks during a

Above: Tim Lincecum had the worst month of his career in August. *Carlos Avila Gonzalez | San Francisco Chronicle*

season. With the Giants, it happened at once. The schedule might have played a part. After an Aug. 1 home win against the Dodgers, the Giants had only one day off before Thursday. In between were two taxing trips through Colorado and Atlanta, then Philadelphia and St. Louis.

All that aside, understanding the 5.20 starters' ERA for August requires a dissection:

— Lincecum (0-4, 8.38 ERA in August) – His struggles have become national news. After an All-Star first half (9-4, 3.16 ERA), his velocity tumbled, his mechanics broke down, his mound presence and conditioning were questioned and he tried a new hand-over-head delivery. Nothing worked. In Saturday's 5-1 loss at St. Louis, Lincecum seemed to take his own advice, stopped overanalyzing and just pitched. The first four innings were his best the entire month, a positive sign. How quickly he lost it in the fifth and sixth, not so much.

— Zito (0-3, 6.26) – Those numbers, which include Wednesday's loss in relief, are troubling for a traditionally strong second-half pitcher. The stuff is there, but often the location is not. For a guy who does not throw hard, that can be deadly. In three of his four starts this month, he has allowed four or more runs. The best sign: only seven walks in 23 innings this month, which shows he is not nitpicking. He just needs to do a better job of hitting corners.

— Cain (2-2, 2.76) – He has been terrific in August, aside from one bad pitch in Philadelphia that resulted in a three-run homer after an error extended the inning. No worries here.

— Sanchez (2-2, 4.23) – Same old, same old. He has some of the best stuff in the league. He gets a ton of swings and misses but cannot string together two quality starts. He ended the starters' winless drought by shoving no-hit stuff at the Phillies for eight innings on the road. Next time out, he could not last five innings to qualify to win a 16-5 game against the Reds at home. The Giants need him to toughen mentally down the stretch. The stuff will take care of itself.

— Bumgarner (1-1, 6.15) – He is a 21-year-old rookie, so anything the Giants get is gravy. He won a week ago by holding the Cardinals to two runs in seven innings. In his next start Wednesday he coughed up eight runs in 2 2/3 innings against the Reds. That is what 21-year-olds in the majors do.

The starters' road should get easier. The Giants have four more off days between now and season's end, which means more rest for weary arms. Aside from the Padres, the Giants have no first- or second-place teams left on their schedule. Hot weather should not be a factor because their three remaining games east of Denver are night games in Chicago. The offense looks as though it can carry more weight, releasing pressure on the starters to be perfect.

The conditions are ripe. Now, it's just a matter of execution.■

Buster Posey reacts in the top of the third after Drew Stubbs scored on an error by pitcher Madison Bumgarner.
Lea Suzuki | San Francisco Chronicle

TIM LINCECUM

ACE IS BACK; JUST DON'T ASK WHY

BY SCOTT OSTLER

Baseball is hard. We have all invested much time and energy in our search for what's wrong with Tim Lincecum.

Now we have to do a U-turn and start figuring out what's right.

Tuesday evening Lincecum laid some of the old Big Time Timmy Jim on the Diamondbacks, striking out 11 in his 6 2/3 innings of work in the 6-3 win.

That's two excellent Cy Young-ish starts in a row, following his monthlong August train wreck.

"To me, he pitched as good as he's pitched (all season)," manager Bruce Bochy said. "The (good) Timmy that we know."

Lincecum didn't even fade in the heat. The Diamondbacks opened their sliding roof to let in the 97-degree (game-time temp) evening heat. Lincecum, instead of wilting, as per his rep, countered with some severe heat of his own.

Now we have to start peeling that onion again, examining layers of clues to find the secret of his new success. It's truly mysterious. For a month Lincecum was lost; for two starts he's been a genius. Has he been staying at a Holiday Inn Express?

Whatever the difference, it's not the hair. Cross that off the list. When Lincecum was struggling, a certain segment of Giants' fandom was sure that Lincecum's hair, creeping down toward his shoulders, was flying around and distracting him.

Lincecum did get a couple of inches trimmed off the length since his previous start, and I asked him after Tuesday's game if that might help explain his big game.

"No," he said with a smile, "it's still (flying) everywhere."

OK, then, what about any adjustments to his between-starts conditioning and throwing routine? Many, including Phillies pitcher Roy Oswalt, speculated that Lincecum had not conditioned himself properly in the offseason.

Was it too late? Apparently not. Lincecum has made some changes, with positive effect.

"I'm becoming more strict on what I do, conditioning and weight-training," Lincecum said. "You

Above: Tim Lincecum rests in the dugout in between innings.
Chad Ziemendorf | San Francisco Chronicle

start pushing yourself and working a little bit harder, because you want to have a little gas left in the tank."

Lincecum, in the first inning Tuesday, was hitting 91-93 mph on the radar gun with his fastball. He stayed in that range, hitting 94 once, and was still throwing 92 in the seventh. So maybe the between-starts tweaking is paying off.

During Bad August, Lincecum seemed to sink into a funk of critical-self analysis, to the point where pitching coach Dave Righetti felt the need to give him a pep talk. Back then, Lincecum would speak of the mental demons creeping into his head.

Now he seems to have found an island of serenity, or sanity. Whether it's the cause of his revitalized pitching, or the result of it, is anyone's guess.

"I've tried to be a little bit more even-keeled the

last two outings," Lincecum said.

Lincecum, as they say, pounded the zone Tuesday. He walked nobody and never threw three balls to a hitter. He retired the first 13 Arizona batters before Miguel Montero's single. Then Lincecum sat down the next five hitters, three on swinging strikeouts.

It was Lincecum's first double-figures strikeout game since July 7, and his second-best K game of the year (13 Marlins, May 4). The whiffs are significant, because Lincecum is now 15-1 lifetime when he strikes out 10 or more. He's a power pitcher.

Bochy, Lincecum and catcher Buster Posey all talked about rhythm. Tim's got rhythm, who could ask for anything more? "Getting his breaking ball (curves and sliders) over for strikes is the big key," Posey said.

Maybe Brian Sabean should get an assist? After the Aug. 28 game – an 11-3 loss in which Barry Zito lasted just 3 2/3 innings – the Giants' general manager gathered four starters in Bochy's office (Matt Cain had left the park early, with permission), and aired them out. Told them, essentially, they weren't getting it done and they'd better go figure it out.

Since then, the starters have yielded 3, 1, 1, 1, 4, 4, 0, 0 and 3 runs. Pretty solid stuff.

Could it be that Sabean, a former Yankees employee, channeled some old George Streinbrenner manhood-challenging?

Lincecum indicated the little chat may have helped. Didn't hurt.

"It just kind of wakes you up," he said, "lights a fire under your butt. It's like my dad used to tell me, it takes a little whomping to wake me up. You understand the severity of every game."

Lincecum is a veteran, but he's only 26. Maybe he's still learning, and growing.

He is pitching better. If you want to know exactly why, just ask your pizza-delivery guy, or your mail carrier, or your mother-in-law, or ...■

HUMBLE ROOKIE'S STELLAR SEASON HITS NEW HEIGHTS AT WRIGLEY FIELD

BY BRUCE JENKINS

Wrigley Field is a haven for the imagination. Hanging around the batting cage Tuesday, I could have sworn I saw Bill Terry, the storied New York Giants first baseman. He was talking to Gabby Hartnett about how the Cubs pitched Babe Ruth in the 1932 World Series. Then Mel Ott leaned in, eager to hear anything about the great Bambino.

Just when the conversation was getting good, the three men vanished, into a fine mist that later turned to rain. And I was jolted back to reality by the comical sight of Tim Lincecum, strolling across the field toward the Giants' dugout, wearing one of those orange Buster Posey giveaway jerseys from AT&T Park.

"I'm his biggest fan," Lincecum said with a goofy grin, only he wasn't kidding.

It has reached the point where if Posey doesn't win the National League's Rookie of the Year award, the voters simply aren't paying attention. Jason Heyward is having a tremendous year in the Braves' outfield, and St. Louis pitcher Jaime Garcia was shutting down the league's best hitters until his arm reached the point of fatigue, perhaps shelving him for the rest of the season.

Posey is simply in another world.

This was his signature game, a 1-0 victory over the Cubs that began with the magnificence of Matt Cain, pitching six innings of two-hit ball, and finished as Posey's complete resume. He caught a shutout, finished by the Giants' bullpen. With his cannon-like arm, he gunned down Cubs shortstop Starlin Castro (another impressive rookie) trying to steal. Then he homered in the eighth, a shot to dead center field off Cubs reliever Andrew Cashner, to provide the game's only run.

After the game, writers from both cities rushed to the Giants' clubhouse to get the latest word on Posey. "You mean Jesus?" asked Aubrey Huff, pronouncing it hay-soos. "Baffling. That's all I can say. I'm baffled by a guy this young, this good."

Posey himself couldn't have been more boring - one of his finest postgame qualities. He hates talking about himself, doesn't really answer any questions regarding his budding greatness, and the beautiful part is, he means it. That's why he has fit so neatly into a clubhouse built upon respect, laughter, cool heads and humility.

I mean, the Giants were going to like the

Above: Rookie catcher Buster Posey adjusted in stride to the major leagues. *Charles Rex Arbogast | AP Photo*

kid, anyway. Hell, he might be the team's most valuable player, let alone a top rookie. But for him to be so down-to-earth, this young, this good, is wondrous to behold.

Posey did mention that as he developed as a hitter at Florida State, he paid particular attention to Matt Holliday and Manny Ramirez, a couple of fearsome right-handed hitters who had extraordinary patience and used the entire field, routinely firing shots to right and center. In that vein, Tuesday night's homer was typical Posey. After a first-pitch strike, he worked his way into a hitter's count by taking the next three pitches for 3-1.

At that point, he said, "I had to be thinking" fastball. And that's what he got. Head down, weight back, bat coiled to strike until the last possible moment, Posey unleashed his latest masterpiece of plate discipline.

"You know, I hate to bring Barry Bonds' name into this," coach Ron Wotus said, "but that's the kind of intelligence this kid has at the plate. The first time I saw him, I knew he was a hitter. Just the patience, the total lack of fear with two strikes, the kind of stuff you can see right away. And to me, the way he calls a game, at his age (23), is even more impressive. You always have to wonder if you can win a division with a rookie catcher, but he's done such a solid job with our staff."

Cain became the latest member of that staff to pitch superbly in the late-September pressure cooker, engaging Carlos Zambrano in a six-inning power duel that had all the old-school tradition of Wrigley's ivy-covered walls and the L train clattering alongside Addison Street.

Here, though, is the true beauty of Wrigley Field, and how it connects the past and present: You really can drift back in time, if you release your mind to the fanciful. Back in that 1932 World Series, Game 3, Ruth took a moment to step out of the batter's box and point toward the center-field bleachers. Historians still debate whether he was merely gesturing or calling his shot, but he hit Charlie Root's next pitch out of the park to dead center.

Tuesday night, a young San Francisco catcher named Posey stood in the same spot, on the exact same field, and home-red to that very part of the yard. His biggest fans are everywhere.∎

Right: Buster Posey (center) had a signature game at Wrigley Field. *Charles Rex Arbogast | AP Photo*

CAIN HAS CURE, SENDS S.F. HOME IN 1ST

BY HENRY SCHULMAN

Padres closer Heath Bell dropped the gauntlet on Twitter the other day when he said, "We want SF in the end. We win and they win then we see who's on top."

Looks like that's the way it's going to be.

The Giants leap- frogged San Diego again for first place in the National League West on Sunday by beating Colorado 4-2. For the umpteenth time in a season that now includes 88 wins, matching last year's total, the Giants quickly forgot a harrowing loss and stormed back with a win.

The Giants' final road game of 2010 was a Matt Cain special. He carried a perfect game into the fifth inning and stood five outs from a no-hitter when Jay Payton legged out an infield hit to short on a ball that Juan Uribe misplayed. Cain, undeterred, completed a three-hitter that left the Rockies all but out of the playoff picture.

The Giants lead the Padres by a half-game. The Rockies are 4 ½ games out of first place and four behind San Diego for the wild card. With a week to go, all signs point to a Padres-Giants dogfight.

"We're right where we want to be. We control it all," first baseman Aubrey Huff said.

Cain was the perfect man to engineer the game that followed Saturday's extra-inning loss. He has not lost since Aug. 18, and the team had won 11 of his prior 13 starts. He is pitching with supreme confidence and thought he had what it took to throw the second no-hitter ever at Coors Field.

"I felt I had good enough stuff," he said. "I felt I had enough oomph left to get the ball down in the zone and throw the ball where I wanted."

Cain cost himself a shot at perfection when he speared Troy Tulowitzki's leadoff grounder in the fifth and bounced a throw to first that Huff could not handle. Cain also issued his only walk in the inning, to Ryan Spilborghs, but struck out Payton and Miguel Olivo to strand the runners.

Cain still had a no-hitter after Spilborghs grounded out to start the eighth. Payton, still quick at 37, hit a grounder up the middle. Uribe was shaded to pull and ran a long way to reach the ball, but he could not pull it out of his glove cleanly, allowing Payton to beat the throw with ease. Uribe, whose error cost Jonathan Sanchez a shot at a perfect game last year, took the fall for Payton's single.

Above: Matt Cain delivers during a gem against the Padres. *Chris Schneider | AP Photo*

"If I don't make a mistake like that, he's out," Uribe said.

Asked if he was disappointed about not getting the no-hitter, Cain said, "I couldn't care less. We needed a win today."

Melvin Mora hit a pinch homer later in the eighth to halve a 4-0 Giants lead. In the ninth, Cain allowed a one-out single by Carlos Gonzalez but forced a pop-up from Tulowitzki. Cain finished his fourth complete game of 2010 with a curveball that Jason Giambi took for strike three.

"Pinpoint accuracy," catcher Buster Posey said of Cain. "It was one of those games when he didn't miss a spot. The swings you saw were pretty indicative of that. It makes my job pretty easy when he has the type of command he had. When I wanted the ball down, it was down. When I wanted the ball up, it was up."

Cain next gets the ball against San Diego on Saturday, near the end of what promises to be a tough final week.

Before the Padres visit San Francisco, the Giants must tackle Arizona, which won two of three at AT&T Park at the end of August.

The final week might have been tougher still had the Giants not taken four of six on their final trip.

"You come in here and get two wins, you take it," Bochy said. "It makes for a real nice road trip. We needed it in our situation, and we got it done."∎

Right: Giants infielder Freddy Sanchez.
Chris Schneider | AP Photo

ROOKIE PITCHER HAS THE POISE

BY GWEN KNAPP

After Madison Bumgarner earned his first home win Thursday, the word "wasn't" somehow became the definitive postgame comment on his work.

"It wasn't pretty," Bumgarner said almost apologetically.

"Madison," Giants manager Bruce Bochy said, pausing to search for the proper way to assess his starting pitcher, "wasn't quite as sharp today."

How wonderfully spoiled this team has become.

No one should expect a 21-year-old to start a game in the last week of a pennant race, place himself in constant trouble and wriggle out of it repeatedly. When most rookies would have been exhaling into a paper bag and then overreaching for their scariest fastball, Bumgarner was throwing off-speed pitches that flummoxed the Diamondbacks. He forced them to maroon baserunners repeatedly in the Giants' 4-1 win.

But on a club with the best ERA in the majors and a staff that every playoff team wants to avoid, Bumgarner's line (five innings and 85 pitches, one run, seven hits, one walk, one hit batter and seven strikeouts) merited only grudging praise. On a roster with Buster Posey, the preternaturally focused Rookie of the Year candidate, poise in a first-year player has become the standard.

Bumgarner helped build those expectations, too. He finished his rookie regular season with a 7-6 record and a 3.00 ERA, and his last month yielded a 1.13 ERA. If the Giants make the playoffs, he has a strong case for a spot in the postseason rotation. Aside from pure numbers, where he has an advantage over Barry Zito, the Giants' lone starter with play-off experience, Bumgarner seems more self-possessed on the mound than both of his lefty colleagues, Zito and Jonathan Sanchez.

In a few short months, he has deftly fixed the mechanical problems that persuaded the Giants to send him to Fresno after spring training instead of following through on plans to make him their fifth starter. He also adjusted the attitude that led to a three-game suspension in the minors after teammates had to restrain him from going after the second-base umpire.

"He had a pretty good snap," Bochy said of the outburst, "and I'm sure he'll have another one. As easy-going as he is, when he's out

Above: Giants starting pitcher Madison Bumgarner. *Michael Macor | San Francisco Chronicle*

there, he's into it."

On the mound these days, Bumgarner tends to look unflappable. Steve Decker, who managed him in the minors, said that outward calm didn't come easily.

"In the minor leagues, if a guy tried to bunt (for a base hit) on him, he'd throw at him," Decker said. "We'd say: 'You can't do that, Madison. The guy's a .200 hitter; how else is he supposed to get on? Don't take it personal.'"

He doesn't think that Bumgarner has been tamed. His intensity has simply been reshaped for public consumption.

"Inside, there's an emotional battle going on, but he's not letting you see it," Decker said. "He's just now able to control it. When he's pitching, he has what I call an animal personality, like Kevin Brown."

It still reveals itself in certain gestures, Decker said, explaining delicately: "I see it every time he blows the snot out of his nose, like a big bull, you know, a raging bull."

He can't help smiling when he talks about the rangy lefthander, whom the Giants took with the 10th pick in the 2007 amateur draft.

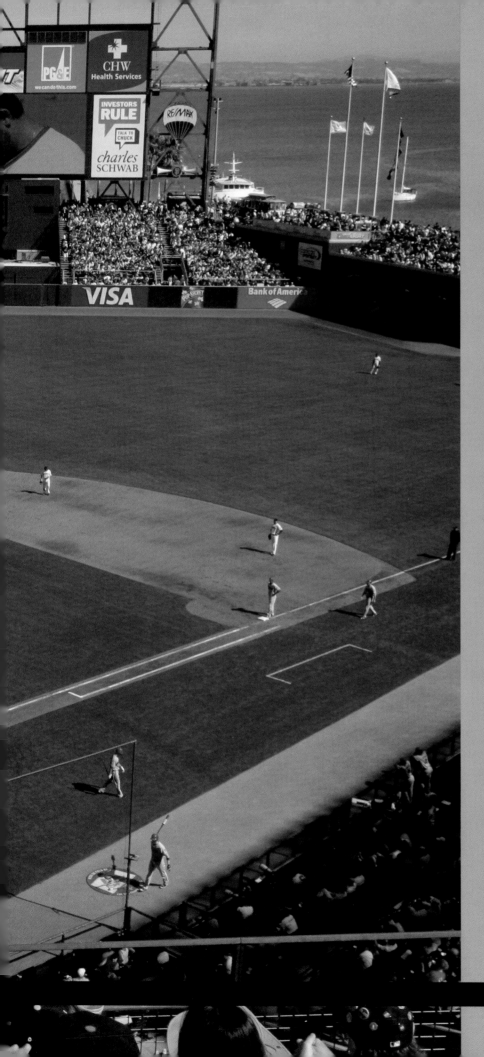

Neither can Jeremy Affeldt. The reliever invited Bumgarner and his wife of seven months, Ali, to stay at his Alamo house during the last homestand. Affeldt wanted company while his wife stayed in Spokane, Wash., after the birth of their second child.

Bumgarner was, to say the least, a resourceful houseguest.

"He practiced roping cows by roping my lawn furniture," Affeldt said. "He's good at it. I'd come home and he'd be spinning this rope. He's lassoing all my furniture. Then he wants to make me walk this weird, funky walk while he's trying to lasso my foot."

Back home in Hudson, N.C., Bumgarner competes in team roping with Ali's father and brother. He said he tried to teach Affeldt, an avid outdoorsman, some tricks, "but that didn't turn out so good."

All the pitchers have mentored him in some way, Bumgarner said, but Affeldt and Matt Cain have taken special care of him. "They'll take me places, and they pay for everything," he said. "I try to offer to pay, but they won't let me."

On Monday, despite not being pretty or sharp, this rookie paid off for all his teammates. ∎

Left: Giants fan Hayden Roberts celebrates a strikeout against the Arizona Diamondbacks.
Paul Chinn | San Francisco Chronicle

POSTSEASON'S GREETINGS

BY HENRY SCHULMAN

Call them what you will: The Freak or The Franchise, Big Daddy and Huff Daddy, B-Weezy and Buster Ballgame, Pat the Bat and the Panda, oooh-REE-bay and Andres the Giant, Sanchy and Sanchy.

Just remember to call them 2010 National League West champions.

The Giants own the title for the first time since 2003 after beating San Diego 3-0 on Sunday in the final game of the regular season, after two difficult losses to the Padres. How else could it be for a team whose unofficial motto was "Giants Baseball: Torture"?

"This is one of the best days of my life," first baseman Aubrey Huff said after he finally got to taste beer that was poured onto his head instead of into a glass. Huff was a sponge soaking up the sounds and sights of his first clinching party, which beat the alternative. Had the Giants lost, they would have been forced to play a tie-breaking game in San Diego today.

"We weren't looking forward to that mental grind on the plane," Huff said. "We didn't want to do that. That team over there gave us a hard time all year. They gave me a heart attack."

Indeed, San Diego won the season series against the Giants 12-6, which might make it harder for the Padres to understand why they will be watching the playoffs from home. The Giants eliminated them and Atlanta won the wild card.

The Giants finished 92-70 and took their seventh West championship since divisional play began in 1969, their first under manager Bruce Bochy and first in the post-Bonds era. Bochy was optimistic it would happen Sunday. He instructed his players not to bring suitcases to the ballpark.

The Giants will host Atlanta in Games 1 and 2 of a best-of-five Division Series on Thursday and Friday, both set to begin at 6:37 p.m. Atlanta was not on the Giants' minds Sunday. Celebrating was.

"I'm just stuttering my words right now, I'm so excited," Tim Lincecum said, happy he does not have to climb the mound at Petco Park today. "We knew it was going to come down to the last day of the season."

How fitting that Jonathan Sanchez was such an important part of the clinching victory after he boldly, and some would argue foolishly, predicted the Giants would sweep a series against the Padres in August, assume first place and not look back. His roadmap might have been off, but he got the destination right.

The fans and media traded Sanchez a zillion times, though general manager Brian Sabean refused to pull the trigger. With a 2009 no-hitter against San Diego already in

Above: Freddy Sanchez, Aaron Rowand, Madison Bumgarner, Buster Posey and the rest of the Giants greet the crowd after the victory.
Brant Ward | San Francisco Chronicle

his pocket, Sanchez on Sunday established himself as a big-game pitcher and assured he will be a key component of the postseason rotation.

Over the final week, Bochy flopped his other four starters to achieve desirable matchups. Only Sanchez was not touched. Game 162 was his.

"He's the guy we wanted out there," Bochy said. "He was throwing as well as anybody. He's had some great games against San Diego," though Bochy acknowledged he had a good fail-safe in Lincecum had the Giants lost.

Sanchez not only carried a shutout into the sixth inning, he also ignited the offense with his first career triple, against Mat Latos, with one out in the third inning. Bochy wanted Sanchez to take the first pitch but could not relay the sign in time to third-base coach Tim Flannery, not that it would have mattered.

"I wasn't taking," Sanchez said, explaining the Padres had been throwing him first-pitch fastballs the whole season, so he came to the plate ready to swing even if he was 7-for-56.

With two outs, Freddy Sanchez lined a single up the middle that scored the pitcher and gave the Giants a crucial run. They were 64-19 this season when they scored first.

Huff then sliced the first pitch to the wall past a diving Chris Denorfia into left-center for a double that brought Freddy Sanchez home for a 2-0 lead.

"The biggest hit of my life," Huff said. "I was walking on air."

How fitting that Buster Posey, whose ascent as the everyday catcher spearhead-ed the Giants into contention, produced the Giants' final run of the regular season when he led off the eighth inning with his 18th homer, off a reliever (Luke Gregerson) who had frustrated San Francisco hitters to no end this year.

How fitting that a bullpen that did not allow an earned run after Sept. 15, sealed the division title. Santiago Casilla, Ramon Ramirez, Sergio Romo and Javier Lopez got the ball to Brian Wilson, who complet-ed the clinching with a 1-2-3 save.

Go figure.

"When he ran the count to the first hit-ter to 3-2, I said, 'Oh, he's going to play around here,'" Bochy joked.

The playing around began when Wilson blew a high 0-2 fastball past the swing of Will Venable to end it. The closer calmly turned toward center field for his custom-ary crossed-arms gesture then swiveled back to find Posey climbing him.

Players flew out of the dugout to form a mob of joy that wound up on the infield dirt near first base. Pablo Sandoval and Juan Uribe shared a ferocious chest-bump before they reached the pile. There were no injuries.

Bochy stayed back in the dugout, hugged his coaches and finally emerged with two fists pumping the air while Sandoval raced to be the first player to grab a championship T-shirt from a bin that had been wheeled to the mound.

Right: Manager Bruce Bochy turns to the bullpen after ending Jonathan Sanchez's day in the sixth inning.
Paul Chinn | San Francisco Chronicle

Above: Manager Bruce Bochy celebrates the NL western division championship with fans. *Paul Chinn | San Francisco Chronicle*

Lower Left: Jacob Castiglionia goes wild as the Giants score . *Chad Ziemendorf | San Francisco Chronicle*

Lower Right: Closer Brian Wilson celebrates the final out. *Paul Chinn | San Francisco Chronicle*

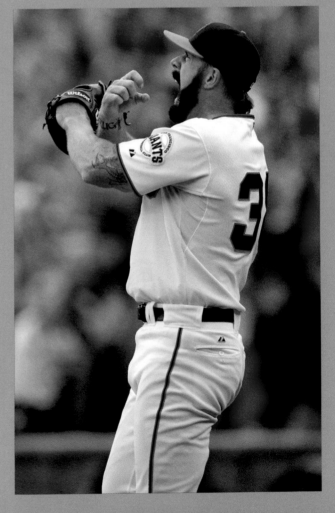

Above: A San Francisco Giant fan shows his feeling. *Lacy Atkins | San Francisco Chronicle*

A crowd of 42,822, who waved orange rally towels at key points in the game and throughout the ninth, thoroughly enjoyed a scene that had not unfolded on this field for seven years. At Bochy's suggestion, Pat Burrell gathered the team for a hands-slapping victory lap around the warning track. Thanking the fans came first, the beer and Champagne second.

"You get to see what the fans were like, how invested they are in this team," Lincecum said. "Some fans were not letting go of my hand. That's why I used my left one."

Lincecum's right hand becomes very important now. He anchors a pitching staff that threw its 17th shutout Sunday and will be asked to carry the team to 11 more wins. Many did not believe the Giants would get this far. Their general manager had a hunch.

"I started to believe when you just started to see the temperament of the club," Sabean said. "They were determined, strong-willed. You could use the word even-keeled. They knew what they needed to do against the clock."

Everyone knew it would go to the final hour. For the organization and its fans, it was worth the wait.■

BUSTER POSEY

GROUNDED BY HIS SOUTHERN ROOTS

BY GWEN KNAPP

At the Leesburg city line on State Route 32, a sign welcomes people to the hometown of country music artist Luke Bryan. The population total sits just under 3,000, yet another young celebrity has already emerged from this verdant stretch of south Georgia.

"Back in August, when he came in with the Giants for the first time, that sign should probably have said: Leesburg closed. Gone to Atlanta to see Buster," said Rob Williams, the high school's baseball coach.

As the Giants return to Georgia for the playoffs today, this pocket of Braves country, a three-hour drive from Atlanta, has largely flipped its loyalties to Buster Posey. It's not just because the catcher is a leading candidate for Rookie of the Year and one of their own – born and bred in Leesburg, married to his high school girlfriend, Kristen, and a homeowner in one of the town's newer developments.

Talk to anyone here, or in the Giants' organization, and you'll hear the same thing: Posey does everything the right way. At 23, he has more maturity and poise than the average 40-year-old, a mind that never quits and a profound discomfort with calling attention to himself. "It's a real credit to how he was raised," Giants manager Bruce Bochy said. "His parents did a great job."

Traci and Demp Posey won't claim a sliver of that credit. They describe their first-born as innately focused, a detail-oriented boy who never needed to be told to clean his room or do his homework, and now a young man who unfailingly remembers to call his grandparents on their birthdays.

Buster's mother said his efficiency did not come from her. "Last-minute was invented for me, " she said.

But an outsider can easily spot resemblances. Buster's description of his ungainly stolen base during Game 1 of the playoffs – "It was a beautiful slide, wasn't it?" – suggests that he inherited his mother's self-deprecating sense of humor.

Buster has two younger brothers, Jack, a redshirt junior on Florida State's baseball team, and

Above: Catcher Buster Posey sits out of a late season game with a sprained forearm. *John Sebastian Russo | San Francisco Chronicle*

17-year-old Jess, still playing for Lee County High. Their sister, Sam, is a junior at Valdosta State, playing third base on the softball team.

"I still think Sam is the most athletic of them," Demp Posey said. "She has the most tools. Buster, I think he's just the hardest worker."

Both parents accommodate requests to discuss their increasingly famous son, but they tend to talk of him as one of their four children, not the superstar, and as part of a team with Kristen. "He's a grown man now with his own life, " Traci said. "We just gave birth to him."

A working environment

But they also raised him in an environment that valued work, and not just as a means to an income or outward success. The Poseys explained their own jobs with deep feeling.

Above: Aubrey Huff, right, put his arm around Buster Posey after a Posey home run. *Brant Ward | San Francisco Chronicle*

Demp Posey is the general manager and a part owner of ACC Distributors Inc., a food-distribution company that employs about 60 people. He has worked his way up in the company over 25 years, he said, often rising at 4 a.m. so he could take afternoon breaks to coach his kids or attend their games. At 49, he said, he has no interest in slowing down. The business has expanded substantially, bringing in $30 million, and he'd like to multiply that.

"It's hard to find a company anymore that keeps growing and doesn't sell out to corporate giants," he explained. "And every time you see a company bought out, you lose jobs."

Traci Posey teaches at Leesburg's Transitional Learning Center, an alternative public school for students with discipline or academic problems. Buster has been surrounded by educators in his family. His paternal grandmother was the principal of the town's primary school, and Kristen's mother worked as a counselor at the same school where his mother once taught sixth-graders.

"I love teaching all sorts of children, but I think this is really my niche," Traci Posey said of the learning center. "If you can keep one kid from dropping out of school and feeling worthless, it's so rewarding."

Buster's success in baseball helps her create a connection with certain students. She assures them that none of his accomplishments – whether at Florida State, or as a No. 5 draft pick working his way through the minors and then a San Francisco rookie – has come easily. She has tapped her son for a couple of classroom talks.

Recently, after a friend gave her a copy of a USA Today story on Buster and teammate Andres Torres, she read the story aloud to her students. She didn't focus on her son. Torres' discussion about his ADHD diagnosis and medication seemed more pertinent.

"A lot of my students who have to take the medication don't like it because it makes them feel weird," she said. "It was great to hear (Torres) talking about how much it helped him."

Lee County is mad for baseball, with so many Little Leaguers that finding practice space can be difficult. Years ago, the Poseys converted part of their home's 50 acres into a batting cage, complete with backstop and pitching screen. Other kids regularly joined the four Posey offspring, plus Demp, in the revamped yard.

A tornado destroyed the backstop a few years ago, dumping an oak tree on top of it, but Traci will always remember the cage fondly for sparing the family miles of carpooling.

SHORTSTOP AND PITCHER

At Lee County High, Buster distinguished himself as both a shortstop and pitcher, throwing fastballs that peaked at 95 mph on the team's radar gun, Williams said. But, like Posey's father, the coach did not see raw talent as Buster's defining trait.

"Most kids want to practice the things that they already do well, " the coach said. "The difference with Buster is that he wanted to work on the things that aren't as much fun, where he really needed to improve."

When Florida State decided to convert him to catcher, Williams said, Buster returned to Leesburg over winter break and practiced blocking wild pitches. The same diligence applied to academics. Buster ranked fourth in his high school class, and his mother remembers him dutifully studying calculus during a national junior team trip to Taiwan.

"A lot of people think he's really quiet," his father said, "but he's really just always listening and learning. I ran into a guy about three weeks ago who coached him when he was 5 or 6, and he said: 'I tell people that's the little joker I put at first base and couldn't get him to say anything, couldn't get a word out of him.' He's sizing things up all the time. I can see it now when they show him in the dugout on TV."

In the past off-season, Kristen would sometimes join her husband at batting cages, throwing to him, or shagging flies in the outfield when he hit with an ex-teammate from Florida State. She attended Auburn right after high school, but eventually transferred to Valdosta State, placing her closer to Buster in Tallahassee.

After dating for close to five years, they married in January 2009. She and her mother slipped an ode to Buster's profession into the ceremony. As the newlyweds walked back up the aisle after exchanging vows, the traditional recessional march had been replaced with "Take Me Out to the Ballgame."

This summer, he has been big news back home. Jim Quinn, editor of the weekly Leesburg Ledger, said the TV station in nearby Albany routinely led its sports report with updates on Buster's 21-game hitting streak in June. Just the other day, he said, a woman came by the newspaper office to hand off a copy of a Buster story that had appeared in the San Diego paper.

Quinn is also Leesburg's mayor, and last year, he and the town council declared a Buster Posey Day, handing him a key to the city.

"It was one of those big fake-looking things," Quinn said. "We had a pep rally for him, and he went to talk at the schools. We'll dedicate a day to him anytime."

A GIANT HOMECOMING

The Giants' playoff visit to Atlanta might inspire another emptying of Leesburg, if enough people can get tickets. Williams already has his, for Monday's game, and he and his wife plan to cut short a trip to the mountains for the occasion.

The Poseys can't make it out to San Francisco. Their jobs and commitments to Buster's three siblings (Jack is getting married after Thanksgiving) preclude the trip out West, but they're planning to go to Atlanta. For Demp, it

Above: Buster Posey looks for confirmation on an out at home plate.
John Sebastian Russo | San Francisco Chronicle

will be only the sixth time he has ever attended a professional baseball game.

Until he went to Philadelphia for Buster's first call-up last year, he had never been to a major-league game. Growing up on a farm about 30 miles from Leesburg, he said, he had to fit most of his activities into an agricultural lifestyle. He played basketball, not baseball, because the sport covered the winter months. Good weather wasn't seen as an invitation to play sports.

When he and Traci moved into their home, it still had remnants of a working farm, mostly cows and horses. For a short time there, Traci and a neighbor raised dairy heifers. Eventually, though, the livestock yielded to a more domestic variety – five dogs and five cats.

Despite the nomadic lifestyle of a young ballplayer, Kristen said, she and Buster couldn't resist adopting two dogs of their own: a springer spaniel and miniature Australian shepherd. The elder is named Chapin, after a beach on Cape Cod, where Buster played in a summer league, and "he has probably traveled more than most people have," Kristen said. The younger one is Chula.

A visit to Leesburg on a sunny day in October revealed lush greenery everywhere, and virtually no traffic at 5 p.m. Though the farmland has gradually morphed into to a bedroom community for nearby Albany, it's still a very different world from San Francisco. But the Posey family has a small link to the Bay Area, established long before the Giants drafted Buster.

His mother grew up as an Army child, and when she was about 6, her father was stationed in the Presidio. That connection won't justify a sign at the city limits, calling Posey a native son. But like Leesburg, the baseball fans of San Francisco seem prepared to dedicate a lot of days to him.

HOW BUSTER GOT HIS NAME

Buster Posey's mother constantly hears that her son has the perfect name for baseball. The nickname, however, has nothing to do with sports. It's a family heirloom, a gift from the great-grandmother of the Giants' star rookie.

He is the third Gerald Dempsey Posey, named for his father and grandfather. As a little boy, his father received the nickname Buster from his grandmother, and it held up for several years, after which the family called him Demp. When his first son and namesake came along, Demp sentimentally requested that they call him Buster for a while.

Realizing that the nickname invited teasing, Traci Posey said, she and her husband assured their son that they'd switch over to a grown-up name when he wanted.

"In first or second grade, our guy came and said: 'I think I'm ready to be called Demp now,'" his mother said. "And we just poked him and said: 'Sorry, but you're Buster.'" ∎

BY A WHISKER
ANOTHER THRILLER GIVES GIANTS 1ST PLAYOFF-SERIES WIN SINCE 2002

BY HENRY SCHULMAN

Fan or player, rookie or old hand, all who watched and participated in the Giants' second clinching celebration in nine days surely had the same thought: "We could get used to this."

"It's contagious," closer Brian Wilson said as he stood awash in Champagne yet again. "It's an addiction we don't want to kick."

For now, the Giants don't have to. They are going to their fifth National League Championship Series after coming from behind twice to beat Atlanta 3-2 Monday night and win their Division Series three games to one. Game 1 of the NLCS will be Saturday in Philadelphia.

Madison Bumgarner, the youngest Giant ever to pitch in a postseason game, again showed steely calm in his six innings and beat 37-year-old postseason pro Derek Lowe. Cody Ross, the accidental Giant, homered to end Lowe's no-hitter in the sixth inning, then singled home the go-ahead run in the seventh, his fourth big hit in a series defined by pitching and defense.

Three shutout innings by relievers Santiago Casilla, Javier Lopez and Brian Wilson set off an on-field celebration that was somewhat subdued, as the Braves were honoring Bobby Cox after his final game as manager.

The clubhouse, though, was another madhouse of flying liquids, chest bumps and backslaps.

Been-there, done-that teams like the Yankees sniff at Division Series clinchers, but the Giants, eight years removed from their last postseason-series win, held nothing back.

"We weren't even thinking what kind of celebration it was going to be," Lopez said. "Obviously, you know it matters. You can see it in here. This is an important time and a big stage for a lot of these guys. It never gets old."

Of course, manager Bruce Bochy aged another year over the four games of this series. All were decided by one run, and Wilson provided a familiar scare when he walked Rick Ankiel and pinch-hitter Eric Hinske with one out in the ninth before he put it away.

"Willie was probably watching in the dugout to see if I was moving around," Bochy said. "I took a seat for a while. I said, 'You're not going to do it to me, Willie. I'm not going to let you get me.'"

Fifteen minutes later, Bochy's players were getting him good with Champagne and beer.

Bumgarner became legal only 71 days earlier, becoming the youngest pitcher to start a postseason game since Kansas City's Bret Saberhagen in 1984. He surrendered a third-inning run on a Brian McCann sacrifice fly.

After Ross tied the game with his homer in the sixth, Bumgarner needed one pitch to fall behind again. He hung a curveball to McCann, who homered for a 2-1 Atlanta lead.

Above: San Francisco Giants congratulate one another after a win over the Atlanta Braves. *AP Photo | Dave Martin*

Bumgarner admitted to some nerves in the first inning. Those evaporated quickly. After the game, he again said that pitching in the North Carolina high school championship game helped him prepare for this. Seriously.

Catcher Buster Posey said Bumgarner's effort at age 21 "is as good sign to come for many years. His composure is unbelievable."

Bumgarner was done after six and won because the Giants scored the go-ahead runs in the seventh-inning small-ball rally.

With one out, Aubrey Huff walked and Posey hit an infield single. Cox visited the mound, where Lowe talked him into facing one more hitter, Pat Burrell. Cox's last crucial managerial decision backfired. Lowe walked Burrell to load the bases.

Juan Uribe, 1-for-13 in the series, tied the game off reliever Peter Moylan with a grounder into the hole at short. Alex Gonzalez fielded it, spun and fired to second, but umpire Ed Hickox ruled the throw pulled second baseman Omar Infante off the bag. Huff scored the tying run, and the bases were still loaded.

Lefty Jonny Venters came on to strike out pinch-hitter Aaron Rowand for the second out before Ross grounded a single to left to give the Giants a 3-2 lead. Burrell tried to score behind Posey but was thrown out.

Ross had the only RBI in the Giants' 1-0 Game 1 victory. He also tripled and scored in the Game 2 loss before delivering his two big hits Monday. Not a bad series for a guy the

Giants really did not want. They claimed him on waivers from Florida to keep him from going to San Diego.

"Who would have thought it?" Ross said with a huge smile. "I don't think even the Giants thought the Marlins would not pull me back (from waivers). Hey, the past is the past. I'm happy to be here and enjoy the ride."

That ride became a rollercoaster after Lopez struck out Jason Heyward to end the eighth with Nate McLouth on second base. Wilson retired the first hitter in the ninth before issuing the two walks. Wilson then struck out Infante, and Melky Cabrera ended the game with a grounder to Uribe. In one more excruciating moment, Uribe's throw sailed, but Travis Ishikawa pulled it down with his foot on the bag.

That launched a party on the same spot in which the Giants celebrated their only other Division Series win, in 2002. They then beat the Cardinals for the pennant and went to their first World Series in 13 years.

The road toward the 2010 World Series begins against the two-time defending NL champs in Philly on Saturday with a matchup between Tim Lincecum, who struck out 14 in his Division Series start and Roy Halladay, who trumped Lincecum with a no-hitter against the Reds.

Wilson, asked if he would pay to see that matchup, said with a straight face, "No, they pay me to see it."∎

Right: Tim Lincecum walks off the mound after striking out the side.
Carlos Avila Gonzalez | San Francisco Chronicle

Above: Fans in the upper deck cheer and wave rally towels during the opening ceremonies. *Chad Ziemendorf | San Francisco Chronicle*

Below: Buster Posey steals second base as Atlanta's Brooks Conrad defends. *Brant Ward | San Francisco Chronicle*

Above: Braves Brian McCann reacts after striking out swinging. *Carlos Avila Gonzalez | San Francisco Chronicle*

Above: Cody Ross singles home Buster Posey with two out in the fourth inning for the game's only run. *Brant Ward | San Francisco Chronicle*

Opposite Page Upper: Cody Ross (13) and Pablo Sandoval do the jump-and-bump for an audience at the conclusion of the Giants' victory. *Paul Chinn | San Francisco Chronicle*

Opposite Page Lower: Fans react in the bottom of the eighth inning. *Lea Suzuki | San Francisco Chronicle*

BOX SCORE

GIANTS 1, BRAVES 0

Braves	AB	R	H	BI	BB	SO	Avg.
O.Infante 3b	4	0	1	0	0	0	.250
Heyward rf	3	0	0	0	1	2	.000
D.Lee 1b	4	0	0	0	0	3	.000
McCann c	3	0	1	0	0	1	.333
Ale.Gonzalez ss	3	0	0	0	0	1	.000
M.Diaz lf	3	0	0	0	0	1	.000
Conrad 2b	3	0	0	0	0	2	.000
Ankiel cf	3	0	0	0	0	1	.000
D.Lowe p	2	0	0	0	0	2	.000
Venters p	0	0	0	0	0	0	-
Hinske ph	1	0	0	0	0	1	.000
Moylan p	0	0	0	0	0	0	-
M.Dunn p	0	0	0	0	0	0	-
Kimbrel p	0	0	0	0	0	0	-
Totals	29	0	2	0	1	14	

Giants	AB	R	H	BI	BB	SO	Avg.
A.Torres cf	4	0	1	0	0	1	.250
F.Sanchez 2b	4	0	0	0	0	0	.000
A.Huff 1b	3	0	1	0	1	1	.333
Posey c	4	1	2	0	0	1	.500
Burrell lf	3	0	0	0	0	2	.000
Schierholtz rf	0	0	0	0	0	0	-
Uribe ss	2	0	0	0	1	1	.000
Sandoval 3b	2	0	0	0	1	1	.000
C.Ross rf-lf	2	0	1	1	1	0	.500
Lincecum p	2	0	0	0	0	2	.000
Totals	26	1	5	1	4	9	

LINESCORE

Braves	000	000	000	-	0	2	2
Giants	000	100	00x	-	1	5	0

E-Ankiel (1), Conrad (1). LOB-Atlanta 3, Giants 6. 2B-O.Infante (1), McCann (1), Posey (1). RBIs-C.Ross (1). SB-Posey (1). CS-A.Huff (1). S-Lincecum. Runners moved up-Ale.Gonzalez. GIDP-F.Sanchez, Sandoval. DP-Atlanta 2 (Conrad, Ale.Gonzalez, D.Lee), (Ale.Gonzalez, Conrad, D.Lee).

Braves	IP	H	R	ER	BB	SO	NP	ERA
D.Lowe L, 0-1	5-1/3	4	1	1	4	6	96	1.69
Venters	1-2/3	0	0	0	0	2	13	0.00
Moylan	1/3	0	0	0	0	2	2	0.00
M.Dunn	0	1	0	0	0	0	5	-
Kimbrel	2/3	0	0	0	0	1	6	0.00

Giants	IP	H	R	ER	BB	SO	NP	ERA
Lincecum W, 1-0	9	2	0	0	1	14	119	0.00

M.Dunn pitched to 1 batter in the 8th. Inherited runners-scored-Venters 2-0, Kimbrel 1-0. IBB-off D.Lowe (Sandoval).

Umpires-Home, Dana DeMuth; First, Paul Nauert; Second, Paul Emmel; Third, Mike Winters; Right, Ed Hickox; Left, Jerry Layne.

Time-2:26. Attendance-43,936 (41,915).

Above: Buster Posey, left, and Pablo Sandoval collide while chasing a pop fly. *Paul Chinn | San Francisco Chronicle*

Right: Aubrey Huff squats down after being called out at second base in a double play to end the bottom of the 10th inning. *Michael Macor | San Francisco Chronicle*

Opposite Page Upper: Brian Wilson is alone with his thoughts in the Giants' dugout after a top of the eighth in which the Braves rallied for three runs to tie the game, with their final two runs of the inning coming on Alex Gonzalez's double off Wilson. *Mike Kepka | San Francisco Chronicle*

Opposite Page Bottom: Pat Burrell is greeted by Juan Uribe after hitting a 3-run home run in the first inning. *Michael Macor | San Francisco Chronicle*

BOX SCORE

BRAVES 5, GIANTS 4

Braves	AB	R	H	BI	BB	SO	Avg.
O.Infante 3b-2b	5	0	2	0	1	2	.333
J. Heyward rf	5	0	0	0	0	2	.000
D. Lee 1b	5	2	2	0	0	1	.222
B. McCann c	4	1	2	1	1	1	.429
M. Cabrera lf	5	0	1	0	0	1	.000
B.Conrad 2b	4	0	1	0	0	1	.143
B. Wagner p	0	0	0	0	0	0	.000
K. Farnsworth p	0	0	0	0	0	0	.000
Ale. Gonzalez ss	5	0	1	2	0	0	.125
R. Ankiel cf	5	1	2	1	0	1	.250
T. Hanson p	1	0	0	0	0	1	.000
N. McLouth ph	1	0	1	0	0	0	1.000
M. Dunn p	0	0	0	0	0	0	.000
P. Moylan p	0	0	0	0	0	0	.000
E. Hinske ph	1	0	0	0	0	0	.000
J. Venters p	0	0	0	0	0	0	.000
M. Diaz ph	1	0	0	0	0	1	.000
C. Kimbrel p	0	0	0	0	0	0	.000
T. Glaus 3b	1	0	0	0	0	0	.000
D. Hernandez 3b	0	0	0	0	0	0	.000
Totals	43	5	11	5	2	11	

Giants	AB	R	H	BI	BB	SO	Avg.
A. Torres cf	4	0	0	0	0	2	.125
F. Sanchez 2b	4	1	1	0	0	2	.125
A. Huff 1b	4	0	0	0	1	3	.143
B. Posey c	4	1	1	0	1	1	.375
Pat . Burrell lf	3	1	2	3	0	0	.333
N. Schierholtz pr-rf	2	0	0	0	0	0	.000
J. Uribe ss-3b	5	0	1	0	0	2	.143
P. Sandoval 3b	4	0	1	0	0	1	.167
R. Ramirez p	0	0	0	0	0	0	.000
T. Ishikawa ph	1	0	0	0	0	0	.000
C. Ross rf-lf	5	1	1	0	0	1	.286
M. Cain p	2	0	1	1	0	1	.500
J. Lopez p	0	0	0	0	0	0	.000
A. Rowand ph	1	0	1	0	0	0	1.000
S. Romo p	0	0	0	0	0	0	.000
B. Wilson p	0	0	0	0	0	0	.000
M. Fontenot 3b	0	0	0	0	0	0	.000
E. Renteria ph-ss	1	0	1	0	0	0	1.000
Totals	40	4	10	4	2	13	

LINESCORE

Braves	000	001	030	01	– 5 11 0
Giants	310	000	000	00	– 4 10 2

Braves	IP	H	R	ER	BB	SO	NP	ERA
T. Hanson	4	5	4	4	1	5	1	9.00
M. Dunn	1.1	0	0	0	0	2	0	0.00
P. Moylan	0.2	1	0	0	0	1	0	0.00
J. Venters	1	2	0	0	0	1	0	0.00
C. Kimbrel	2	0	0	0	0	4	0	0.00
B. Wagner	0.1	1	0	0	0	0	0	0.00
K. Farnsworth w, 1-0	1.2	1	0	0	1	0	0	0.00

Giants	IP	H	R	ER	BB	SO	HR	ERA
M. Cain	6.2	7	1	0	2	6	0	0.00
J. Lopez	0.1	0	0	0	0	1	0	0.00
S. Romo	0	2	2	2	0	0	0	0.00
B. Wilson	2	1	1	0	0	3	0	0.00
R. Ramirez L, 0-1	2	1	1	1	0	1	1	4.50

Umpires: Home - Paul Nauert, First Base - Paul Emmel, Second Base - Mike Winters, Third Base - Jerry Layne

Above: Starting pitcher Jonathan Sanchez. *Jamie Squire | Getty Images*
Opposite Page: Giants' Freddy Sanchez reacts after scoring the go-ahead run on a Buster Posey ground ball. *John Bazemore | AP Photo*

BOX SCORE

GIANTS 3, BRAVES 2

Giants	AB	R	H	BI	BB	SO	Avg.
A.Torres cf	4	0	1	0	1	1	.167
F.Sanchez 2b	4	1	1	0	1	1	.167
A.Huff 1b	5	0	2	1	0	1	.250
Br.Wilson p	0	0	0	0	0	0	-
Posey c	4	0	2	0	1	1	.417
Burrell lf	2	0	0	0	1	1	.250
Schierholtz rf	2	0	1	0	0	1	.250
Uribe ss	4	0	0	0	0	1	.091
Fontenot 3b	4	1	1	0	0	1	.250
C.Ross rf-lf	4	0	0	0	0	0	.182
J.Sanchez p	3	0	0	0	0	2	.000
Romo p	0	0	0	0	0	0	-
Ishikawa ph-1b	0	1	0	0	1	0	.000
Totals	36	3	8	1	5	10	

Braves	AB	R	H	BI	BB	SO	Avg.
O.Infante 3b	4	0	0	0	0	1	.231
Heyward rf	4	0	0	0	0	3	.000
D.Lee 1b	3	0	0	0	1	1	.167
McCann c	4	0	1	0	0	2	.364
D.Ross pr	0	0	0	0	0	0	-
M.Diaz lf	3	0	0	0	0	0	.000
McLouth cf	1	0	0	0	0	0	.500
Ale.Gonzalez ss	3	1	1	0	0	2	.182
Conrad 2b	3	0	0	0	0	1	.100
Ankiel cf	2	0	0	0	0	1	.200
Glaus ph	0	0	0	0	0	0	.000
Hinske ph	1	1	1	2	0	0	.333
Kimbrel p	0	0	0	0	0	0	-
M.Dunn p	0	0	0	0	0	0	-
Moylan p	0	0	0	0	0	0	-
Farnsworth p	0	0	0	0	0	0	-
T.Hudson p	2	0	1	0	0	1	.500
Venters p	0	0	0	0	0	0	-
Me.Cabrera ph-lf	1	0	0	0	0	0	.000
Totals	26	1	5	1	4	9	

LINESCORE

Giants	010	000	002	-	3	8	0
Braves	000	000	020	-	2	4	3

E-Conrad 3 (4). LOB-Giants 11, Atlanta 3. 3B-Fontenot (1). HR-Hinske (1), off Romo. RBIs-A.Huff (1), Hinske 2 (2). SB-A.Torres (1). CS-A.Torres (1). Runners moved up-A.Torres. GIDP-Uribe. DP-Atlanta 1 (O.Infante, Conrad, D.Lee).

Giants	IP	H	R	ER	BB	SO	NP	ERA
J.Sanchez	7-1/3	2	1	1	1	11	105	1.23
Romo W, 1-0 BS, 1-1	2/3	1	1	1	0	0	10	40.50
Br.Wilson S, 1-2	1	1	0	0	0	1	18	0.00

Braves	IP	H	R	ER	BB	SO	NP	ERA
T.Hudson	7	4	1	0	4	5	106	0.00
Venters	1	2	0	0	0	3	20	0.00
Kmbrl L, 0-1 H, 1	2/3	1	2	1	1	1	19	2.70
M.Dunn BS, 1-1	0	1	0	0	0	0	2	0.00
Moylan	0	0	0	0	0	0	4	0.00
Farnsworth	1/3	0	0	0	0	1	5	0.00

M. Dunn pitched to 1 batter in the 9th. Moylan pitched to 1 batter in the 9th. Inherited runners-scored-Romo 1-1, M.Dunn 2-1, Moylan 2-1, Farnsworth 2-0.

Umpires-Home, Paul Emmel; First, Mike Winters; Second, Jerry Layne; Third, Ed Hickox; Right, Paul Nauert; Left, Dana DeMuth.

Time-3:23 Attendance-53,284 (49,743).

Atlanta Braves catcher Brian McCann (16) tags out San Francisco Giants' Pat Burrell at the plate during the seventh inning of Game 4. *Dave Martin | AP Photo*

Above: Giants pitcher Madison Bumgarner. *John Bazemore | AP Photo*

Opposite Page: Atlanta Braves Jason Heyward slides safely into second base on a throwing error as San Francisco Giants second baseman Freddy Sanchez (21) flies overhead. *John Amis | AP Photo*

Opposite Page (inset): Atlanta Braves manager Bobby Cox waves to fans. Cox is retiring. *Dave Martin | AP Photo*

BOX SCORE

GIANTS 3, BRAVES 2

Giants	AB	R	H	BI	BB	SO	Avg.
A.Torres cf	4	0	0	0	0	2	.125
F.Sanchez 2b	4	0	0	0	0	0	.125
A.Huff 1b	3	1	1	0	1	1	.267
Br.Wilson p	0	0	0	0	0	0	-
Posey c	4	1	1	0	0	2	.375
Burrell lf	2	0	0	0	1	1	.200
S.Casilla p	0	0	0	0	0	0	-
Ja.Lopez p	0	0	0	0	0	0	-
Ishikawa ph-1b	1	0	0	0	0	0	.000
Uribe ss-3b	3	0	0	1	0	1	.071
Fontenot 3b	2	0	0	0	0	1	.167
Rowand ph	1	0	0	0	0	1	.500
Schierholtz rf	0	0	0	0	0	0	.250
C.Ross rf-lf	3	1	2	2	0	1	.286
Bumgarner p	2	0	0	0	0	0	.000
Renteria ss	1	0	1	0	0	0	1.000
Totals	30	3	5	3	2	11	

Braves	AB	R	H	BI	BB	SO	Avg.
O.Infante 2b	5	1	1	0	0	2	.222
M.Diaz lf	3	0	1	0	0	0	.100
Me.Cabrera ph-lf	2	0	0	0	0	0	.000
D.Lee 1b	4	0	0	0	0	1	.125
McCann c	3	1	2	2	0	0	.429
McLouth pr	0	0	0	0	0	0	.500
D.Ross c	0	0	0	0	0	0	-
Ale.Gonzalez ss	4	0	1	0	0	2	.200
Heyward rf	4	0	2	0	0	1	.125
Glaus 3b	3	0	0	0	0	1	.000
Venters p	0	0	0	0	0	0	-
Kimbrel p	0	0	0	0	0	0	-
Conrad ph	1	0	0	0	0	0	.091
Ankiel cf	2	0	0	0	2	1	.167
D.Lowe p	2	0	0	0	0	0	.000
Moylan p	0	0	0	0	0	0	-
Di.Hernandez 3b	1	0	0	0	0	1	.000
Hinske ph	0	0	0	0	1	0	.333
2-T.Hudson pr	0	0	0	0	0	0	.500
Totals	34	2	7	2	3	9	

LINESCORE

Giants	000	001	200	-	3	5	1
Braves	001	001	000	-	2	7	2

E-Fontenot (1), Ale.Gonzalez 2 (2). LOB-Giants 2, Atlanta 9. HR-C.Ross (1), off D.Lowe; McCann (1), off Bumgarner. RBIs-Uribe (1), C.Ross 2 (3), McCann 2 (3). CS-A.Torres (2). SF-McCann. Runners moved up-D.Lee, Ale.Gonzalez. GIDP-F.Sanchez, Ishikawa. DP-Atlanta 2 (Ale.Gonzalez, O.Infante, D.Lee), (Ale.Gonzalez, D.Lee).

Giants	IP	H	R	ER	BB	SO	NP	ERA
Bumgarner w, 1-0	6	6	2	2	1	5	85	3.00
S.Casilla H, 1	1-2/3	1	0	0	0	2	23	0.00
Ja.Lopez H, 2	1/3	0	0	0	0	1	4	0.00
Br.Wilson S, 2-3	1	0	0	0	2	1	25	0.00

Braves	IP	H	R	ER	BB	SO	NP	ERA
D.Lowe L, 0-2	6-1/3	2	3	2	2	8	101	2.31
Moylan BS, 1-1	0	0	0	0	0	0	5	0.00
Venters	1-2/3	3	0	0	0	2	26	0.00
Kimbrel	1	0	0	0	0	1	7	2.08

Moylan pitched to 1 batter in the 7th. Venters pitched to 1 batter in the 9th. Inherited runners-scored-Ja.Lopez 1-0, Moylan 3-1, Venters 3-1, Kimbrel 1-0.

Umpires-Home, Mike Winters; First, Jerry Layne; Second, Ed Hickox; Third, Dana DeMuth; Right, Paul Nauert; Left, Paul Emmel.

Time-2:56   Attendance-44,532 (49,743).

COACH BRUCE BOCHY

BOCHY'S CAP SIZE, HE HAS ALL THE RIGHT MOVES

BY SCOTT OSTLER

Man, if you thought Bruce Bochy had a big head before ...

After Tuesday afternoon's 3-0 win over the Phillies, when every move the Giants' manager made turned to solid-gold bullion, Bochy should look like Jack, in those Jack in the Box TV commercials.

Of course, that's not Bochy. You rip him, he shrugs. You praise him, he shrugs. You snap him with a towel, he shrugs.

Tuesday at 10 a.m., you were ripping him. That's what time Bochy posted his lineup card in the clubhouse. Newspaper beat writers immediately Twittered the much-anticipated lineup to their audiences, and the Twitter-rejoinder network, if that's what it's called, lit up like a nuclear-powered Christmas trees.

Edgar Renteria starting at short, with Juan Uribe at third and Pablo Sandoval on the bench? Is Bochy nuts?

Renteria batting leadoff? Six years ago, sure, but isn't this 2010? He's playing with one arm!

Pat Burrell moved up to the cleanup spot? Does Bochy know Burrell is hitting .235 this postseason?

One pictured Bochy's critics as a howling mob with torches and pitchforks, on roller skates in case Bochy tried to make a break for it.

Well, the critics had a terrible day.

Renteria hit a leadoff single in the fourth to break up Cole Hamels' perfect game and kick off a two-run rally.

Cody Ross, whom many armchair managers would have penciled into the leadoff spot instead of the five-hole, had a two-out single that inning to drive in the first – and winning – run. Bochy didn't want Ross at leadoff because he's been driving in runs.

Aaron Rowand? Many critics didn't like the idea of him replacing Andres Torres in centerfield, but the much-maligned Rowand, long a Bochy favorite, led off the fifth with a double and scored the third run.

What else?

Matt Cain, moved back from the No. 2 starting spot to No. 3 so he could start this game at home,

Above: Manager Bruce Bochy.
Carlos Avila Gonzalez | San Francisco Chronicle

was sensational. A 409-foot flyball out by Phils slugger Ryan Howard in the second inning would have been a home run, easy, in Game 2 in Philadelphia.

That wasn't Bruce Bochy out there, that was John McGraw. If you see Bochy in the dugout tonight wearing a 1920s suit and a straw hat, you'll know why.

Bochy moved Burrell into Buster Posey's cleanup spot, and Burrell had what might be the at-bat of the Giants' postseason so far, with all due respect to Cody "The Mashin' Martian" Ross.

Burrell came to bat in the fourth with two outs and runners on first and second. After taking a ball, he swung and missed, then looked at three more balls, two of them on the fringes of the strike zone. Burrell's walk set the table for Cody to unload-y.

Bochy put an exaggerated infield shift on Howard, who grounded out to second baseman Freddy Sanchez in short right field.

Bochy, to use the sanitized version of an old

Above: Pablo Sandoval has a word with manager Bruce Bochy as he waits to bat.
Michael Macor | San Francisco Chronicle

baseball expression, had a horse-shoe in his back pocket Tuesday, except that it wasn't really luck. Tuesday, he was a skipper who knows his ballclub.

Besides, it's not like Bochy had a lot to work with. With the team-wide trend of cooling bats, however Bochy shuffled the pieces, the line-up was going to be Ross and seven flailers. That lineup card was going to look as appetizing as the all-night room-service menu at a cheap hotel.

Bochy wasn't so much steering the ship as he was bailing it out like crazy.

After the game, Bochy declined the opportunity to gloat, when asked if it felt good to see his moves pay off, in the big hits by Renteria and Rowand.

"You feel good for them," Bochy said.

Was his maneuvering a matter of hunches, or desperation, or what?

"Well, I talked about this earlier, " Bochy said. "I know Andres is strug-gling. So I told Aaron to be ready. He was going to be out there today. And with the lefthander (Hamels) going, Edgar was going to play today. ... And with Torres out, Edgar was our best option to lead off, and he did a nice job out there, even his first at-bat," a six-pitch flyout.

Second-guessing Bochy – includ-ing second-guessing him before the fact – has become a favorite pastime of Giants fans. He is fair game, that's part of the deal, Bochy gets paid to do this. And staying with Sandoval and Rowand long after many fans were ready to move on, hey, that stuff is legitimately debat-able.

But by late Tuesday afternoon, the howling mob had fallen silent. Just as well. Like Torres, the mob can use a rest, especially now that it looks as if its members might have to armchair-manage several more games this month.■

CLASSIC GIANTS
URIBE'S HOMER SENDS S.F. TO WORLD SERIES

BY HENRY SCHULMAN

It had to be the first pitch. It just had to be. Could anyone in his right mind picture Juan Uribe letting a half dozen go by before delivering his team a pennant?

Ryan Madson threw a slider, and not a very good one. Uribe pounced. That's what he does. It's in his DNA. In the time it took for his two-out home run in the eighth inning to clear the right-field fence, just barely, and for the fun-loving shortstop to round the bases with his right arm raised, his teammates started to understand they were going to the World Series.

Uribe's first homer in what had been a terrible offensive postseason broke a tie and gave the Giants a 3-2 victory at Citizens Bank Park. They won the National League Championship Series four games to two.

So now this team of misfits and mercenaries will face the Texas Rangers in a World Series that not even the screwiest mind could have conjured when the season began. Game 1 is at AT&T Park on Wednesday.

"It's amazing," first baseman Aubrey Huff said. "The whole world wanted to see the Phillies and Yankees in the World Series, but you know what? It's time for new blood."

The hero is old blood. Uribe won a World Series championship ring in 2005 with the Chicago White Sox. He had some big hits in that postseason, but none as memorable as this.

"This was a big one, like me. Pow!" Uribe said as he broke into laughter in the near-solitude of the weight room as the standard clubhouse mayhem unfolded behind him. "It was for the World Series."

Giants fans long will remember how Uribe stepped to the plate in a hostile stadium, with three hits in 27 at-bats, plus a game-winning sacrifice fly, in the 2010 playoffs, and sent the Bay Area into delirium while stomping on the Phillies, 46,062 fans in the park and everyone else in the land of cheesesteaks.

The Giants captured the 19th modern-era pennant in franchise history and their fourth in San Francisco. They won the NLCS for the third time in five tries since the series was introduced in 1969 and clinched on the road for the first time. It was a pennant few expected, even as the Giants flew to Philadelphia with a 3-2 lead in the series.

"When we lost the last game in San Francisco, everyone was saying, 'We're in trouble. The momentum has swung,' but we found a way to do it," said Bruce Bochy, who goes to his second World Series as a manager. His 1998 Padres were swept by the Yankees.

Befitting this postseason, and for that matter the entire season, the clinching game was intense and bizarre.

Jonathan Sanchez was gone after two-plus innings with two of his runners on base. He walked off the mound slowly, seething, after

Above: A welcoming committee including Pablo Sandoval, Cody Ross and Andres Torres waits for Juan Uribe after his eighth-inning homer.
Lance Iversen | San Francisco Chronicle

he and Phillies second baseman Chase Utley ignited a benches-clearing scrum.

Sanchez threw six consecutive balls to start the third inning before hitting Utley in the back. Utley flipped the ball dismissively toward Sanchez, who took offense. Lip readers might argue that Sanchez yelled, "That's bull-," with Utley responding "What's bull-?" before taking a few steps toward the pitcher.

In an odd sight, the relievers had to run a marathon from the center-field bullpens to join the altercation, the Giants trailing the Phillies because their bullpen was one level higher. They had to descend steps. Jeremy Affeldt was warming up and, in fact, Bochy was going to the mound to yank Sanchez when all heck broke loose.

Affeldt started to run down the steps when bullpen coach Mark Gardner grabbed him.

"He said, 'You stay here. You need to lock it in right now,'" Affeldt said. "'We've got a long game ahead of us, and you need to stay focused.'"

So Affeldt continued to warm up, hearing taunts from fans who called him every feminine epithet in the books for not joining his mates to fight. It was a profound move by Gardner.

Affeldt, who rarely pitched down the stretch and only two-thirds of an inning previously in the postseason, relieved Sanchez, buzzed through Philly's 4-5-6 hitters to strand the two runners, preserved the 2-2 tie and added a perfect fourth.

Affeldt started seven shutout innings by a bullpen that included Madison Bumgarner for two innings, Tim Lincecum for three batters, Javier Lopez and, of course, Brian Wilson.

Pitching coach Dave Righetti praised his entire bullpen but said, "I'm most proud of Jeremy. To me, he was the game."

But there would be no win, no pennant, without a third run, and Uribe provided it against a reliever who struck out six consecutive Giants in one stretch over Games 4, 5 and 6. Uribe got his slider, and the odds he would swing at the first pitch?

"Ninety-eight percent," Matt Cain said.

The Phillies were not done. Wilson needed a line-drive double play to end the eighth and walked a pair in the ninth. Uribe made a stellar play for a force to get the second out, justifying Bochy's decision to have him play third over Pablo Sandoval.

Naturally, Wilson went to three balls on the final three hitters before he struck out Ryan Howard looking to ignite a celebration that stayed on the field for a good while and was years in the making.

This franchise was a wreck in the wake of Barry Bonds' departure. Finally, it appears fixed. Broken teams do not go to the World Series, but hung-over teams do. Good thing there are three days in between.

"It's going to get real weird tonight,"■

Left: The Giants celebrate their victory, Juan Uribe jumps in the center, as San Francisco beats the Philadelphia Phillies 3-2, in game 6.
Michael Macor | San Francisco Chronicle

Above: Philadelphia fan Jason Rush and San Francisco fan Calvin Lui, who are best friends, watch as the teams warm up for game 1.
Michael Macor | San Francisco Chronicle

Left: Aubrey Huff is called off a fly ball by Freddy Sanchez.
Lance Iversen | San Francisco Chronicle

Below: San Francisco Giants manager Bruce Bochy smiles after talking with Phillies manager Charlie Manuel, as the teams prepare for the game.
Lance Iversen | San Francisco Chronicle

BOX SCORE

GIANTS 4, PHILLIES 3

Giants	AB	R	H	BI	BB	SO	Avg.
A.Torres cf	5	0	1	0	0	2	.200
F.Sanchez 2b	5	0	0	0	0	1	.000
A.Huff 1b	4	0	1	0	0	0	.250
Br.Wilson p	0	0	0	0	0	0	-
Posey c	4	1	1	0	0	2	.250
Burrell lf	3	0	2	1	0	1	.667
Schierholtz pr-rf	1	1	0	0	0	1	.000
Uribe ss	4	0	1	1	0	1	.250
Fontenot 3b	4	0	1	0	0	0	.250
C.Ross rf-lf	3	2	2	2	1	0	.667
Lincecum p	3	0	0	0	0	2	.000
Ja.Lopez p	0	0	0	0	0	0	-
Ishikawa 1b	0	0	0	0	0	0	-
Totals	36	4	9	4	1	10	

Phillies	AB	R	H	BI	BB	SO	Avg.
Victorino cf	5	0	0	0	0	2	.000
Polanco 3b	4	0	1	0	0	0	.250
Utley 2b	3	1	1	0	1	0	.333
Howard 1b	4	0	1	0	0	3	.250
Werth rf	3	1	2	2	1	1	.667
Rollins ss	4	0	0	0	0	3	.000
Ibanez lf	3	0	0	0	1	1	.000
C.Ruiz c	3	1	1	1	0	1	.333
2-W.Valdez pr	0	0	0	0	0	0	-
Halladay p	2	0	1	0	0	1	.500
Do.Brown ph	1	0	0	0	0	0	.000
Madson p	0	0	0	0	0	0	-
Lidge p	0	0	0	0	0	0	-
Gload ph	1	0	0	0	0	1	.000
Totals	33	3	7	3	3	13	

LINESCORE

Giants	001	012	000	-	4	9	0	
Phillies	001	002	000	-	3	7	0	

LOB-Giants 7, Philadelphia 7. 2B-Burrell (1), Polanco (1), Howard (1). HR-C.Ross 2 (2), off Halladay 2; C.Ruiz (1), off Lincecum; Werth (1), off Lincecum. RBIs-Burrell (1), Uribe (1), C.Ross 2 (2), Werth 2 (2), C.Ruiz (1). SB-Fontenot (1). GIDP-Victorino. DP-Giants 1 (F.Sanchez, Uribe, A.Huff).

Giants	IP	H	R	ER	BB	SO	NP	ERA
Lincecum W, 1-0	7	6	3	3	3	8	113	3.86
Ja.Lopez H, 1	2/3	0	0	0	0	1	9	0.00
Br.Wilson S, 1-1	1-1/3	1	0	0	0	4	33	0.00

Phillies	IP	H	R	ER	BB	SO	NP	ERA
Halladay L, 0-1	7	8	4	4	0	7	105	5.14
Madson	1	0	0	0	0	1	9	0.00
Lidge	1	1	0	0	1	2	23	0.00

HBP-by Br.Wilson (C.Ruiz), by Lidge (Ishikawa). PB-Posey.

Umpires-Home, Derryl Cousins; First, Dan Iassogna; Second, Ted Barrett; Third, Wally Bell; Right, Tom Hallion; Left, Jeff Nelson.

Time-2:59 Attendance-45,929 (43,651).

NLCS GAME TWO

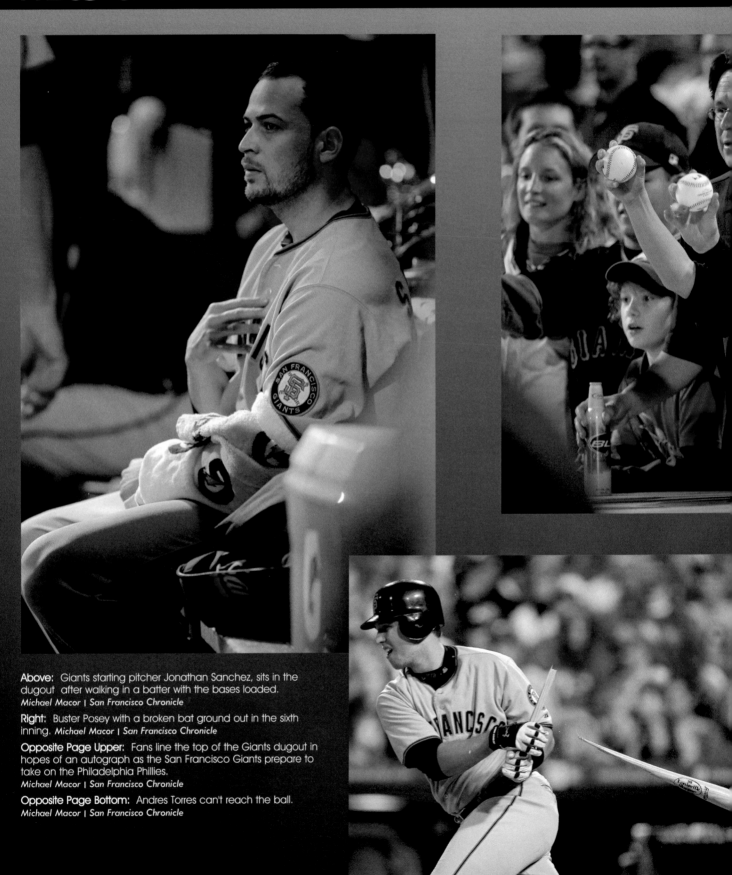

Above: Giants starting pitcher Jonathan Sanchez, sits in the dugout after walking in a batter with the bases loaded.
Michael Macor | San Francisco Chronicle

Right: Buster Posey with a broken bat ground out in the sixth inning. *Michael Macor | San Francisco Chronicle*

Opposite Page Upper: Fans line the top of the Giants dugout in hopes of an autograph as the San Francisco Giants prepare to take on the Philadelphia Phillies.
Michael Macor | San Francisco Chronicle

Opposite Page Bottom: Andres Torres can't reach the ball.
Michael Macor | San Francisco Chronicle

BOX SCORE

PHILLIES 6, GIANTS 1

Giants	AB	R	H	BI	BB	SO	Avg.
A.Torres cf	4	0	0	0	0	4	.111
F.Sanchez 2b	4	0	2	0	0	1	.222
A.Huff 1b	4	0	0	0	0	0	.125
Posey c	3	0	0	0	1	0	.143
Burrell lf	4	0	0	0	0	1	.286
C.Ross rf	3	1	1	1	1	1	.500
Fontenot 3b	2	0	0	0	1	1	.167
S.Casilla p	0	0	0	0	0	0	-
Romo p	0	0	0	0	0	0	-
Ishikawa ph	1	0	1	0	0	0	1.000
Renteria ss	4	0	0	0	0	0	.000
J.Sanchez p	2	0	0	0	0	2	.000
R.Ramirez p	0	0	0	0	0	0	-
Affeldt p	0	0	0	0	0	0	-
Sandoval 3b	0	0	0	0	1	0	-
Totals	31	1	4	1	4	10	

Phillies	AB	R	H	BI	BB	SO	Avg.
Victorino cf	4	1	2	0	0	1	.222
Utley 2b	3	2	0	0	2	1	.167
Polanco 3b	3	1	1	2	0	0	.286
Howard 1b	3	0	2	0	1	1	.429
Werth rf	3	1	0	0	1	2	.333
Rollins ss	3	0	2	4	1	0	.286
Ibanez lf	4	0	0	0	0	2	.000
C.Ruiz c	4	0	0	0	0	2	.143
Oswalt p	3	1	1	0	0	0	.333
Gload ph	1	0	0	0	0	0	.000
Madson p	0	0	0	0	0	0	-
Totals	31	6	8	6	5	9	

LINESCORE

Giants	000	010	000	-	1 4 1
Phillies	100	010	40x	-	6 8 0

E-Fontenot (1). LOB-Giants 7, Philadelphia 8. 2B-Victorino (1), Howard (2), Rollins (1). HR-C.Ross (3), off Oswalt. RBIs-C.Ross (3), Polanco 2 (2), Rollins 4 (4). SB-Utley 2 (2), Polanco (1). S-Victorino. SF-Polanco.

Giants	IP	H	R	ER	BB	SO	NP	ERA
J.Sanchez L, 0-1	6	5	3	2	3	7	100	3.00
R.Ramirez	1/3	1	2	2	1	0	7	54.00
Affeldt	1/3	0	1	1	1	1	9	27.00
S.Casilla	1/3	1	0	0	0	0	6	0.00
Romo	1	1	0	0	0	1	11	0.00

Phillies	IP	H	R	ER	BB	SO	NP	ERA
Oswalt W, 1-0	8	3	1	1	3	9	111	1.13
Madson	1	1	0	0	1	1	22	0.00

J.Sanchez pitched to 1 batter in the 7th. Inherited runners-scored-R.Ramirez 1-1, Affeldt 2-0, S.Casilla 3-3. IBB-off Affeldt (Werth), off R.Ramirez (Utley).

Umpires-Home, Dan Iassogna; First, Ted Barrett; Second, Wally Bell; Third, Jeff Nelson; Right, Derryl Cousins; Left, Tom Hallion.

Above: Soaking in the moment, Chris Zafra, 15, flies his Giants flag in left field. *Mike Kepka | San Francisco Chronicle*

Upper Left: Aaron Rowand scored on a Freddy Sanchez single. *Michael Macor | San Francisco Chronicle*

Lower Left: Pitcher Matt Cain talks with catcher Buster Posey during Game 3. *Lacy Atkins | San Francisco Chronicle*

Below: Giants Pat Burrell, Buster Posey, Brian Wilson and Nate Schierholtz celebrate their win. *Michael Macor | San Francisco Chronicle*

BOX SCORE

GIANTS 3, PHILLIES 0

Phillies	AB	R	H	BI	BB	SO	Avg.
Victorino cf	2	0	0	0	1	0	.182
Utley 2b	4	0	0	0	0	0	.100
Polanco 3b	4	0	0	0	0	1	.182
Howard 1b	4	0	1	0	0	1	.364
Werth rf	3	0	0	0	1	2	.222
Rollins ss	4	0	1	0	0	0	.273
Ibañez lf	4	0	0	0	0	2	.000
C.Ruiz c	2	0	1	0	0	0	.222
Hamels p	2	0	0	0	0	1	.000
Gload ph	0	0	0	0	1	0	.000
Contreras p	0	0	0	0	0	0	-
Totals	29	0	3	0	3	7	

Giants	AB	R	H	BI	BB	SO	Avg.
Renteria ss	4	1	1	0	0	0	.125
F.Sanchez 2b	3	0	1	1	0	0	.250
Posey c	4	0	0	0	0	2	.091
Burrell lf	2	1	0	0	1	2	.222
Schierholtz rf	0	0	0	0	0	0	.000
C.Ross rf-lf	3	0	1	1	0	1	.444
A.Huff 1b	3	0	1	1	0	0	.182
Uribe 3b	3	0	0	0	0	0	.143
Rowand cf	3	1	1	0	0	2	.333
Ja.Lopez p	0	0	0	0	0	0	-
Br.Wilson p	0	0	0	0	0	0	-
M.Cain p	2	0	0	0	0	2	.000
A.Torres ph-cf	1	0	0	0	0	0	.100
Totals	28	3	5	3	1	9	

LINESCORE

Phillies	000	000	000	-	0	3	0
Giants	000	210	00x	-	3	5	0

LOB-Philadelphia 7, Giants 3. 2B-Rowand (1). RBIs-F.Sanchez (1), C.Ross (4), A.Huff (1). SB-Victorino (1). S-F.Sanchez. GIDP-Ibañez. DP-Giants 1 (F.Sanchez, Renteria, A.Huff).

Phillies	IP	H	R	ER	BB	SO	NP	ERA
Hamels L, 0-1	6	5	3	3	1	8	101	4.50
Contreras	2	0	0	0	0	1	24	0.00

Giants	IP	H	R	ER	BB	SO	NP	ERA
M.Cain W, 1-0	7	2	0	0	3	5	119	0.00
Ja.Lopez H, 2	1	0	0	0	0	1	9	0.00
Br.Wilson S, 2-2	1	1	0	0	0	1	10	0.00

HBP-by M.Cain (Victorino, C.Ruiz).

Umpires-Home, Ted Barrett; First, Wally Bell; Second, Jeff Nelson; Third, Tom Hallion; Right, Dan Iassogna; Left, Derryl Cousins.

Time-2:39   Attendance-43,320 (41,915).

Above: Aubrey Huff scores the winning run on a fly ball by Juan Uribe in the bottom of the ninth inning.
Michael Macor | San Francisco Chronicle

Right: Giants players including Freddy Sanchez (center) celebrated the victory. *Lance Iversen | San Francisco Chronicle*

Opposite Page Upper: In a catcher-meets-catcher moment, Buster Posey tags out Carlos Ruiz in the fifth inning after Shane Victorino's single. Posey made a nice short-hop grab of Aaron Rowand's throw, then held onto the ball after the collision with Ruiz. *Lacy Atkins | San Francisco Chronicle*

Opposite Page Bottom: Braxton Rico of Watsonville peers over his hands while watching the bottom of the ninth inning.
Lea Suzuki | San Francisco Chronicle

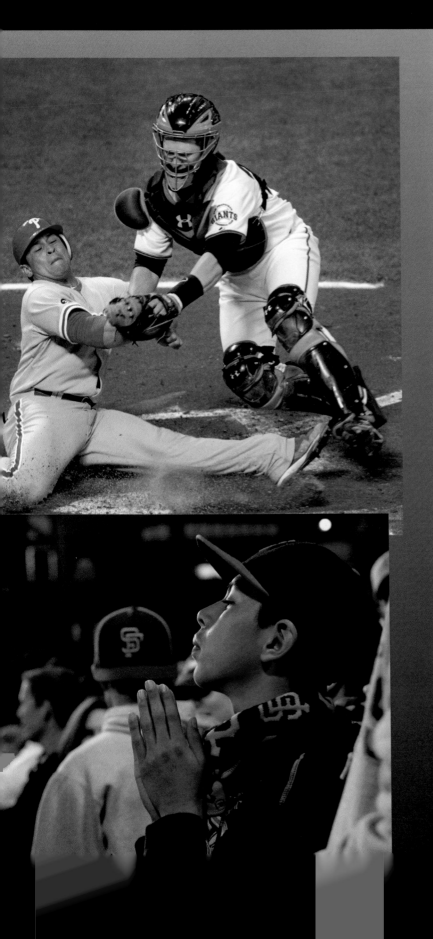

BOX SCORE

GIANTS 6, PHILLIES 5

Phillies	AB	R	H	BI	BB	SO	Avg.
Victorino cf	4	1	1	1	1	2	.200
Utley 2b	5	1	1	0	0	0	.133
Polanco 3b	3	1	2	2	0	0	.286
Howard 1b	2	1	1	0	2	1	.385
Werth rf	3	0	1	1	0	0	.250
Rollins ss	4	0	1	0	0	2	.267
B.Francisco lf	4	1	1	0	0	2	.250
C.Ruiz c	4	0	1	0	0	3	.231
Blanton p	1	0	0	0	0	1	.000
Contreras p	0	0	0	0	0	0	-
Do.Brown ph	1	0	0	0	0	0	.000
Durbin p	0	0	0	0	0	0	-
Bastardo p	0	0	0	0	0	0	-
Madson p	0	0	0	0	0	0	-
Gload ph	1	0	0	0	0	0	.000
Oswalt p	0	0	0	0	0	0	.333
Totals	32	5	9	4	3	11	

Giants	AB	R	H	BI	BB	SO	Avg.
Renteria ss	4	0	0	0	1	1	.083
Br.Wilson p	0	0	0	0	0	0	-
F.Sanchez 2b	5	1	1	0	0	0	.235
A.Huff 1b	5	2	3	1	0	1	.313
Posey c	5	0	4	2	0	1	.313
Burrell lf	2	1	0	0	2	0	.182
Romo p	0	0	0	0	0	0	-
Uribe ss	0	0	0	1	0	0	.143
C.Ross rf-lf	3	1	1	0	0	0	.417
Sandoval 3b	4	0	1	2	0	0	.250
Rowand cf	2	0	0	0	0	1	.200
S.Casilla p	0	0	0	0	0	0	-
Ishikawa ph	1	0	0	0	0	1	.500
Ja.Lopez p	0	0	0	0	0	0	-
Schierholtz rf	1	0	0	0	0	1	.000
Bumgarner p	1	0	0	0	0	1	.000
A.Torres cf	2	1	1	0	1	0	.167
Totals	35	6	11	6	4	7	

LINESCORE

Phillies	000	040	010	-	5 9 1
Giants	101	012	001	-	6 11 0

Two outs when winning run scored. E-Rollins (1). LOB-Philadelphia 6, Giants 9. 2B-Polanco (2), Howard (3), Werth (1), Posey 2 (2), C.Ross (1), Sandoval (1). RBIs-Victorino (1), Polanco 2 (4), Werth (3), A.Huff (2), Posey 2 (2), Uribe (2), Sandoval 2 (2). CS-Rollins (1), A.Torres (1). S-Blanton. SF-Uribe. Runners moved up-Renteria, Sandoval. GIDP-Polanco, Sandoval. DP-Philadelphia 1 (Utley, Rollins, Howard); Giants 1 (F.Sanchez, Renteria, A.Huff).

Phillies	IP	H	R	ER	BB	SO	NP	ERA
Blanton	4-2/3	5	3	3	1	3	63	5.79
Contreras	1/3	0	0	0	0	1	6	0.00
Durbin BS, 1-1	1	2	2	2	2	1	38	18.00
Bastardo	1/3	1	0	0	0	0	10	0.00
Madson	1-2/3	1	0	0	1	2	32	0.00
Oswalt L, 1-1	2/3	2	1	1	0	0	18	2.08

Giants	IP	H	R	ER	BB	SO	NP	ERA
Bumgarner	4-2/3	6	3	3	1	6	85	5.79
S.Casilla	1-1/3	1	1	1	1	2	30	5.40
Ja.Lopez H, 3	1	1	1	1	1	0	16	3.38
Romo BS, 1-1	1	1	0	0	0	2	11	0.00
Br.Wilson W, 1-0	1	0	0	0	0	1	12	0.00

Ja.Lopez pitched to 1 batter in the 8th. Inherited runners-scored-Contreras 1-0, Madson 1-0, S.Casilla 2-2, Romo 1-1. IBB-off S.Casilla (Howard). HBP-by Blanton (C.Ross), by S.Casilla (Werth), by Bumgarner (Polanco). WP-Blanton 2, S.Casilla.

Above: Cody Ross and Buster Posey watch their teammates during the 9th inning and the Philly victory.
Lacy Atkins | San Francisco Chronicle

Right: Fans entering AT&T park. *Liz Hafalia | San Francisco Chronicl*

BOX SCORE

PHILLIES 4, GIANTS 2

Phillies	AB	R	H	BI	BB	SO	Avg.
Victorino cf	5	1	0	0	0	1	.150
Polanco 3b	3	0	1	1	1	0	.294
Utley 2b	4	0	1	0	0	1	.158
Howard 1b	4	0	0	0	0	3	.294
Werth rf	4	1	1	1	0	1	.250
Rollins ss	4	0	1	0	0	1	.263
Ibanez lf	4	1	2	0	0	1	.133
C.Ruiz c	2	1	0	0	1	0	.200
Halladay p	1	0	0	0	0	1	.333
Gload ph	1	0	0	0	0	0	.000
Contreras p	0	0	0	0	0	0	-
J.Romero p	0	0	0	0	0	0	-
Madson p	0	0	0	0	0	0	-
B.Francisco ph	1	0	0	0	0	0	.200
Lidge p	0	0	0	0	0	0	-
Totals	33	4	6	3	2	9	

Giants	AB	R	H	BI	BB	SO	Avg.
A.Torres cf	3	1	2	0	1	0	.267
F.Sanchez 2b	4	0	2	0	0	0	.286
A.Huff 1b	4	0	0	0	0	0	.250
Posey c	3	0	0	1	1	1	.263
Burrell lf	4	1	1	0	0	2	.200
C.Ross rf	4	0	1	1	0	3	.375
Sandoval 3b	4	0	1	0	0	0	.250
Uribe ss	4	0	0	0	0	1	.091
Lincecum p	2	0	0	0	0	1	.000
Fontenot ph	1	0	0	0	0	1	.143
Romo p	0	0	0	0	0	0	-
Ja.Lopez p	0	0	0	0	0	0	-
R.Ramirez p	0	0	0	0	0	0	-
Affeldt p	0	0	0	0	0	0	-
Ishikawa ph	1	0	0	0	0	1	.333
Totals	34	2	7	2	2	10	

LINESCORE

Phillies	003	000	001	-	4	6	1
Giants	100	100	000	-	2	7	2

E-Howard (1), A.Huff (1), Sandoval (1). LOB-Philadelphia 6, Giants 7. 2B-Burrell (2), C.Ross (2). HR-Werth (2), off R.Ramirez. RBIs-Victorino (2), Polanco (5), Werth (4), Posey (3), C.Ross (5). SB-Utley (3), Rollins 2 (2). S-Halladay. DP-Philadelphia 1 (Werth, Werth, Polanco); Giants 1 (A.Huff).

Phillies	IP	H	R	ER	BB	SO	NP	ERA
Halladay W, 1-1	6	6	2	2	2	5	108	4.15
Contreras H, 1	2/3	1	0	0	0	1	11	0.00
J.Romero H, 1	1/3	0	0	0	0	0	3	0.00
Madson H, 1	1	0	0	0	0	3	13	0.00
Lidge S, 1-1	1	0	0	0	0	1	10	0.00

Giants	IP	H	R	ER	BB	SO	NP	ERA
Lincecum L, 1-1	7	4	3	2	1	7	104	3.21
Romo	1/3	0	0	0	1	0	9	0.00
Ja.Lopez	2/3	0	0	0	0	1	9	2.70
R.Ramirez	2/3	2	1	1	0	0	16	27.00
Affeldt	1/3	0	0	0	0	1	6	13.50

Inherited runners-scored-J.Romero 1-0, Ja.Lopez 1-0, Affeldt 2-0. HBP-by Lincecum (C.Ruiz).

Umpires-Home, Jeff Nelson; First, Tom Hallion; Second, Derryl Cousins; Third, Dan Iassogna; Right, Wally Bell; Left, Ted Barrett.

Time-3:15   Attendance-43,713 (41,915).

Aaron Rowand of the San Francisco Giants is doused with beer in the locker room after defeating the Philadelphia Phillies 3-2 in Game Six of the NLCS to advance to the World Series. *Lance Iversen | San Francisco Chronicle*

Above: Jeremy Affeldt works the 5th inning.
Lance Iversen | San Francisco Chronicle

Right: Freddy Sanchez (21) has his bats ready in the dugout.
Lance Iversen | San Francisco Chronicle

Opposite Page Upper: Bruce Bochy, in jacket, visits pitcher Jonathan Sanchez as the umpires huddle after a bench-clearing scuffle in the fourth. *Lance Iversen | San Francisco Chronicle*

Opposite Page Bottom: Phillies' Jayson Werth watches Giants' Juan Uribe's eighth inning home run go over the wall, putting the Giants in the lead. *Lance Iversen | San Francisco Chronicle*

BOX SCORE

GIANTS 3, PHILLIES 2

Giants	AB	R	H	BI	BB	SO	Avg.
A.Torres cf	5	0	3	0	0	2	.350
Rowand cf	0	0	0	0	0	0	.200
F.Sanchez 2b	4	0	3	0	0	1	.360
A.Huff 1b	4	1	1	1	1	2	.250
Posey c	4	0	0	0	1	1	.217
Burrell lf	4	0	1	0	0	1	.211
Lincecum p	0	0	0	0	0	0	.000
Br.Wilson p	1	0	0	0	0	0	.000
C.Ross rf-lf	4	0	1	0	0	0	.350
Uribe 3b	3	1	2	1	0	0	.214
Renteria ss	4	0	0	0	0	1	.063
J.Sanchez p	1	1	1	0	0	0	.333
Affeldt p	0	0	0	0	0	0	-
Fontenot ph	1	0	1	0	0	0	.250
Bumgarner p	0	0	0	0	0	0	.000
Ishikawa ph	1	0	0	0	0	1	.250
Ja.Lopez p	0	0	0	0	0	0	-
Schierholtz rf	1	0	0	0	0	1	.000
Totals	37	3	13	2	2	10	

Phillies	AB	R	H	BI	BB	SO	Avg.
Rollins ss	4	0	1	0	1	1	.261
Polanco 3b	3	1	0	0	2	0	.250
W.Valdez pr	0	0	0	0	0	0	-
Utley 2b	3	1	1	1	1	0	.182
Howard 1b	5	0	2	0	0	3	.318
Werth rf	2	0	0	1	1	1	.222
Victorino cf	4	0	2	0	0	0	.208
Ibanez lf	4	0	2	0	0	0	.211
C.Ruiz c	3	0	0	0	0	1	.167
Oswalt p	2	0	0	0	0	0	.200
B.Francisco ph	1	0	0	0	0	1	.167
Madson p	0	0	0	0	0	0	-
Lidge p	0	0	0	0	0	0	-
Gload ph	1	0	0	0	0	0	.000
Totals	32	2	8	2	5	7	

LINESCORE

Giants	002	000	010	-	3 13 0
Phillies	200	000	000	-	2 8 1

E-Polanco (1). LOB-Giants 11, Philadelphia 11. 2B-F.Sanchez (1), C.Ross (3), Utley (1), Howard (4), Ibanez (1). HR-Uribe (1), off Madson. RBIs-A.Huff (3), Uribe (3), Utley (1), Werth (5). S-F.Sanchez, C.Ruiz. SF-Werth. GIDP-C.Ross, Renteria. DP-Giants 1 (A.Huff, Renteria); Philadelphia 2 (Polanco, Utley, Howard), (Utley, Howard).

Giants	IP	H	R	ER	BB	SO	NP	ERA
J.Sanchez	2	3	2	2	2	1	50	4.50
Affeldt	2	0	0	0	0	2	26	3.38
Bumgarner	2	3	0	0	1	1	26	4.05
Ja.Lopez W, 1-0	1	0	0	0	0	1	12	2.08
Lincecum H, 1	1/3	2	0	0	0	1	16	3.14
Br.Wilson S, 3-3	1-2/3	0	0	0	2	1	26	0.00

Phillies	IP	H	R	ER	BB	SO	NP	ERA
Oswalt	6	9	2	1	0	5	99	1.84
Madson L, 0-1	2	2	1	1	1	3	32	1.35
Lidge	1	2	0	0	1	2	17	0.00

J.Sanchez pitched to 2 batters in the 3rd. Inherited runners-scored-Affeldt 2-0, Br.Wilson 2-0. IBB-off Bumgarner (Werth), off Lidge (Posey), off Madson (A.Huff). HBP-by J.Sanchez (Utley), by Oswalt (Uribe). WP-J.Sanchez.

Umpires-Home, Tom Hallion; First, Derryl Cousins; Second, Dan Iassogna; Third, Ted Barrett; Right, Jeff Nelson; Left, Wally Bell.

Time-3:41   Attendance-46,062 (43,651).

GIANTS WIN IT!
SAN FRANCISCO CELEBRATES FIRST WORLD SERIES TITLE IN CITY'S HISTORY

BY HENRY SCHULMAN

There stood pitcher Matt Cain, at 26 the longest-tenured player on the 2010 Giants, raising the circle-of-flags trophy above his head on the field so hundreds of San Francisco fans who refused to leave the Rangers' ballpark could see it.

"Wow, this is sick," Cain said. "We're the World Series champions of 2010."

How long the faithful have waited to hear those words - not years, but generations. The Giants moved to San Francisco in 1958 and had not touched that trophy until Monday night, when they beat the Texas Rangers 3-1.

The Giants needed only five games to win the franchise's sixth World Series, its first since 1954. They dominated Texas in ways they could not have imagined during a 162-game regular season and two rounds of play-offs that lived up to the team's unofficial motto of "Giants baseball: Torture."

The unlikely Most Valuable Player for an unlikely World Series winner was Edgar Renteria, an injury-plagued shortstop from Colombia who might retire after the season and whose two-year, $18.5 million contract was ridiculed because the Giants gave it to a player thought to be washed up.

Renteria already belonged in the pantheon of World Series heroes. In 1997, then 22 and a big-leaguer for less than two seasons, he won Game 7 for Florida with an 11th-inning single. On Monday, Renteria secured a seat at the head table when he supplied all of the Giants' runs with a three-run homer in the seventh inning that broke a 0-0 tie.

Renteria called his shot against Cliff Lee, twice telling center fielder Andres Torres before the game he was going to go deep.

"He told Andres he was going to hit one and he did it," outfielder Aaron Rowand said. "He Babe Ruth-ed it, I guess."

Tim Lincecum, the two-time Cy Young Award winner, allowed three hits and struck out 10 in eight innings in the most important win of his 26-year-old life.

On a team with so much youth, it was fitting that Buster Posey, a 23-year-old rookie catcher, did the keenest job summarizing what this championship means to an organization and a city that was starved for it.

"It's crazy to think with all the great baseball players who have come through San Francisco, there hasn't been a World Series championship," Posey said.

"The beautiful thing about the organization is, you've got guys like Will Clark here. You've got J.T. Snow here. You've got Shawon Dunston here. When we get back to San Francisco, we'll have Willie Mays and Willie McCovey and Gaylord Perry. The list goes on and on. It's so humbling to have won the first World Series in San Francisco. It's unbelievable."

How fitting that the Series ended with clos-

Above: The Giants celebrate on the field after winning the final game of the World Series. *Carlos Avila Gonzalezo | San Francisco Chronicle*

er Brian Wilson blowing a strike-three fastball past Rangers outfielder Nelson Cruz, setting off a celebration sure to rock the Bay Area for a long time. After all, everyone had generations to plan it.

52 TITLE-FREE YEARS

With the first toast, revelers could bid good riddance to the ghosts of failures past.

McCovey's line drive to Bobby Richardson in 1962, the earthquake sweep in 1989 and the Game 6 collapse in 2002 - their power to spook the faithful is gone, defused by a championship year led by four homegrown pitchers, including Lincecum, who came up huge in the clinching game.

Former managing general partner Peter Magowan, a Giants fan since 1951 who could not guide the franchise to a title during 16 years at the helm, said this title makes up for everything.

"It does. It erases it," Magowan said. "I don't think a day goes by that I don't think about the '02 World Series. I still think a lot about '62, to say nothing about all the other near-misses. This does knock it all away."

NAILING IT DOWN

With two outs in the seventh inning of a 0-0 game, and Cody Ross and Juan Uribe on base after singling, Renteria knocked a 2-0 cut fastball from Cliff Lee over the wall in left-center field for a three-run homer that helped secure the trophy.

First baseman Aubrey Huff, who broke into tears as the World Series win truly dawned on him, said he was happier for Renteria than anyone.

Renteria was derided by fans for not living up to his contract. In 2010, he spent four tours on the disabled list with four different injuries. He was injured in late September when the Giants, who were not hitting, held a pregame meeting inside the batting cage at Wrigley Field.

In one of the season's most emotional moments, according to those who attended, Renteria rose to speak. He was in tears.

"I had a feeling this was going to be my last year," Renteria recounted Monday. "I told my teammates, 'Let's go. Let's play hard. I know we can do it. I believe in you guys. If you guys have a chance to put us in the playoffs, I'll help you once we get there.'

"The Giants organization gave me a two-year contract and I was not able to help them. But they always had my back. I just wanted to do something big for them."

The Giants still had to get nine outs after Renteria's homer. Lincecum got six. Though he allowed a seventh-inning homer by Cruz, he also struck out three hitters in the inning and one more in the eighth.

LINCECUM WAS LIGHTS-OUT

Lincecum was not sharp during the Giants' Game 1 win. In Game 5 he was lights-out and became the 15th pitcher in history to win four games in one postseason.

Posey said he knew it would be OK before the game when he saw Lincecum's demeanor.

"It's called being a gamer, " Posey said. "Walk into the clubhouse today and the guy's as loose as he can be, joking around, same old Timmy. He had no idea he had an opportunity to go out and win Game 5 of the World Series and win us a championship."

Afterward, it still had not sunk in.

"It'll take over later on tonight, " Lincecum said, "when we get to be by ourselves and really think about everything."∎

Above: San Francisco Giants celebrate their first ever San Francisco Giants World Series. *Lance Iversen | San Francisco Chronicle*

Above: Boating Giants fans fill McCovey Cove.
Liz Hafalia | San Francisco Chronicle

Upper Left: Giants Juan Uribe connects for a 3-run homer.
Michael Macor | San Francisco Chronicle

Lower Left: Pitcher Matt Cain talks with catcher Buster Possey during Game 3.
Lacy Atkins | San Francisco Chronicle

Below: Giants Pat Burrell high-fives Juan Uribe, 5, after scoring on an Aubrey Huff single. *Carlos Avila Gonzalez | San Francisco Chronicle*

BOX SCORE

GIANTS 11, RANGERS 7

Rangers	AB	R	H	BI	BB	SO	Avg.
Andrus ss	3	2	1	1	1	1	.333
M.Young 3b	4	0	0	0	1	0	.000
J.Hamilton cf	4	1	0	0	1	0	.000
Guerrero rf	4	0	1	2	0	1	.250
N.Cruz lf	5	0	1	2	0	1	.200
Kinsler 2b	4	1	1	0	1	0	.250
B.Molina c	4	2	2	1	0	1	.500
Moreland 1b	3	0	2	0	0	1	.667
Cantu ph-1b	1	0	0	0	0	0	.000
Cl.Lee p	2	0	1	0	0	0	.500
O'Day p	0	0	0	0	0	0	-
Dav.Murphy ph	1	0	1	1	0	0	1.000
Ogando p	0	0	0	0	0	0	-
M.Lowe p	0	0	0	0	0	0	-
Kirkman p	0	0	0	0	0	0	-
Borbon ph	1	1	1	0	0	0	1.000
Totals	36	7	11	7	4	5	

Giants	AB	R	H	BI	BB	SO	Avg.
A.Torres cf	4	2	1	0	0	2	.250
F.Sanchez 2b	5	2	4	3	0	0	.800
Posey c	5	0	1	1	0	2	.200
Burrell lf	3	1	0	0	1	3	.000
Schierholtz rf	1	0	1	1	0	0	1.000
C.Ross rf-lf	5	1	1	1	0	2	.200
A.Huff 1b	4	1	3	1	0	0	.750
R.Ramirez p	0	0	0	0	0	0	-
Affeldt p	0	0	0	0	0	0	-
Br.Wilson p	0	0	0	0	0	0	-
Uribe 3b	4	1	1	3	0	3	.250
Renteria ss	3	2	1	0	0	0	.333
Lincecum p	3	0	0	0	0	0	.000
S.Casilla p	0	0	0	0	0	0	-
Romo p	0	0	0	0	0	0	-
Ja.Lopez p	0	0	0	0	0	0	-
Ishikawa ph-1b	1	1	1	1	0	0	1.000
Totals	38	11	14	11	1	12	

LINESCORE

Rangers	110	002	003	-	7	11	4
Giants	002	060	03x	-	11	14	2

E-Guerrero 2 (2), M.Young (1), Andrus (1), A.Huff (1), Ishikawa (1). LOB-Texas 8, Giants 6. 2B-N.Cruz (1), B.Molina (1), Moreland (1), Cl.Lee (1), A.Torres (1), F.Sanchez 3 (3), A.Huff (1), Ishikawa (1). HR-Uribe (1), off O'Day. RBIs-Andrus (1), Guerrero 2 (2), N.Cruz 2 (2), B.Molina (1), Dav.Murphy (1), F.Sanchez 3 (3), Posey (1), Schierholtz (1), C.Ross (1), A.Huff (1), Uribe 3 (3), Ishikawa (1). CS-A.Huff (1). SF-Andrus, Guerrero. Runners moved up-J.Hamilton. GIDP-Kinsler. DP-Texas 1 (Kinsler, Andrus); Giants 1 (Uribe, A.Huff).

Rangers	IP	H	R	ER	BB	SO	NP	ERA
Cl.Lee L, 0-1	4-2/3	8	7	6	1	7	104	11.57
O'Day	1/3	1	1	1	0	1	13	27.00
Ogando	2	1	0	0	0	4	25	0.00
M.Lowe	2/3	3	3	3	0	0	23	40.50
Kirkman	1/3	1	0	0	0	0	5	0.00

Giants	IP	H	R	ER	BB	SO	NP	ERA
Lincecum W, 1-0	5-2/3	8	4	4	2	3	93	6.35
S.Casilla H, 1	1-1/3	0	0	0	0	1	19	0.00
Romo	2/3	1	0	0	0	1	7	0.00
Ja.Lopez	1/3	0	0	0	0	0	2	0.00
R.Ramirez	1/3	1	2	2	1	0	12	54.00
Affeldt	0	0	1	1	1	0	6	-
Br.Wilson	2/3	1	0	0	0	0	11	0.00

Affeldt pitched to 1 batter in the 9th. Inherited runners-scored-O'Day 2-2, Kirkman 1-1, S.Casilla 2-0, Affeldt 2-0, Br.Wilson 3-3. HBP-by Cl.Lee (A.Torres), by O'Day (Renteria). WP-Affeldt.

Umpires-Home, John Hirschbeck; First, Sam Holbrook; Second, Bill Miller; Third, Mike Winters; Right, Gary Darling; Left, Jeff Kellogg.

Time-3:36   Attendance-43,601 (41,915).

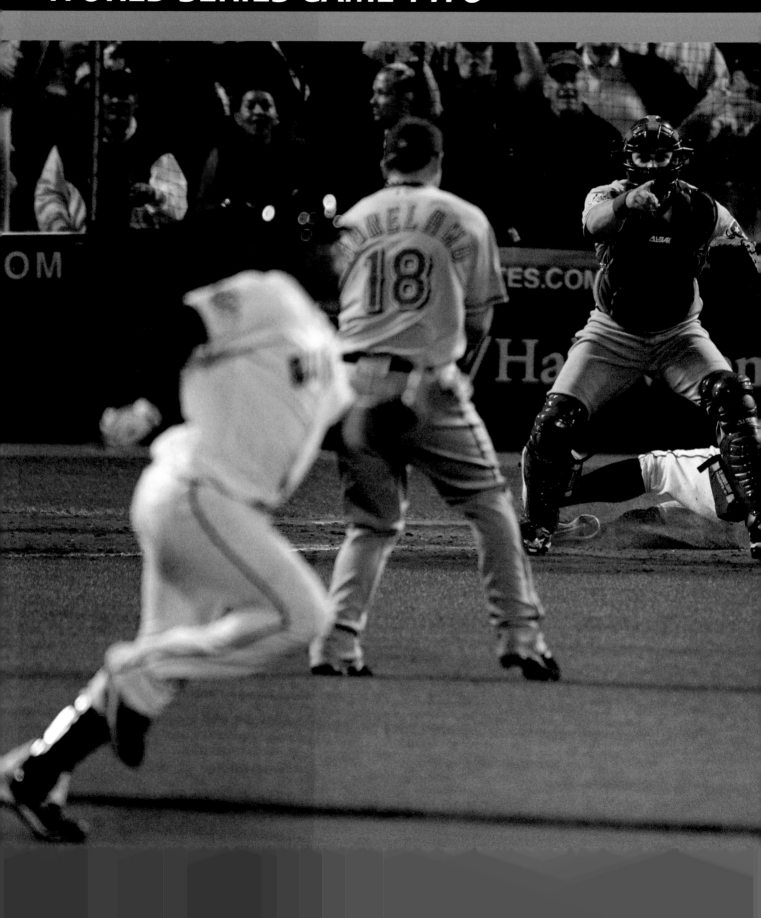

Above: Cody Ross gets a close look at ball four in the eighth inning, the second of four consecutive walks that fueled a seven-run rally and put the game out of reach.
Brant Ward | San Francisco Chronicle

Left: Cody Ross scores on a Juan Uribe single in the seventh. Uribe took second on the throw and was safe.
Carlos Avila Gonzalez | San Francisco Chronicle

Below: Pins on the hat of a fan waiting outside of AT&T park. *Liz Hafalia | San Francisco Chronicle*

BOX SCORE

GIANTS 9, RANGERS 0

Rangers	AB	R	H	BI	BB	SO	Avg.
Andrus ss	3	0	0	0	1	0	.167
M.Young 3b	4	0	1	0	0	0	.125
J.Hamilton cf	4	0	1	0	0	0	.125
N.Cruz rf	4	0	0	0	0	2	.111
Kinsler 2b	4	0	1	0	0	0	.250
Dav.Murphy lf	3	0	0	0	1	0	.250
Treanor c	3	0	0	0	0	0	.000
Francoeur ph	1	0	0	0	0	0	.000
Moreland 1b	2	0	1	0	1	0	.600
C.Wilson p	1	0	0	0	0	0	.000
D.Oliver p	0	0	0	0	0	0	-
Borbon ph	1	0	0	0	0	0	.500
O'Day p	0	0	0	0	0	0	-
D.Holland p	0	0	0	0	0	0	-
M.Lowe p	0	0	0	0	0	0	-
Kirkman p	0	0	0	0	0	0	-
Totals	30	0	4	0	3	2	

Giants	AB	R	H	BI	BB	SO	Avg.
A.Torres cf	5	0	1	1	0	1	.222
F.Sanchez 2b	5	0	0	0	0	2	.400
Posey c	4	1	1	0	0	2	.222
Burrell lf	2	0	0	0	1	1	.000
Schierholtz rf	0	1	0	0	1	0	1.000
C.Ross rf-lf	2	2	1	0	2	0	.286
A.Huff 1b	3	1	0	1	1	0	.429
Uribe 3b	3	1	1	2	1	1	.286
Renteria ss	4	2	2	3	0	1	.429
M.Cain p	3	0	1	0	0	1	.333
Ja.Lopez p	0	0	0	0	0	0	-
Fontenot ph	0	0	0	0	0	0	-
Rowand ph	1	1	1	2	0	0	1.000
Mota p	0	0	0	0	0	0	-
Totals	32	9	8	9	6	9	

LINESCORE

					R	H	E
Rangers	000	000	000	-	0	4	0
Giants	000	010	17x	-	9	8	0

LOB-Texas 7, Giants 5. 2B-Kinsler (1), A.Torres (2), C.Ross (1). 3B-Rowand (1). HR-Renteria (1), off C.Wilson. RBIs-A.Torres (1), A.Huff (2), Uribe 2 (5), Renteria 3 (3), Rowand 2 (2). SB-Andrus (1). S-C.Wilson.

Rangers	IP	H	R	ER	BB	SO	NP	ERA
C.Wilson L, 0-1	6	3	2	2	2	4	101	3.00
D.Oliver	1	1	0	0	0	2	11	0.00
O'Day	2/3	1	1	1	0	2	16	18.00
D.Holland	0	0	3	3	3	0	13	-
M.Lowe	0	1	2	2	1	0	14	67.50
Kirkman	1/3	2	1	1	0	1	12	13.50

Giants	IP	H	R	ER	BB	SO	NP	ERA
M.Cain W, 1-0	7-2/3	4	0	0	2	2	102	0.00
Ja.Lopez H, 1	1/3	0	0	0	0	0	2	0.00
Mota	1	0	0	0	1	0	19	0.00

C.Wilson pitched to 1 batter in the 7th. D.Holland pitched to 3 batters in the 8th. M.Lowe pitched to 2 batters in the 8th. Inherited runners-scored-D.Oliver 1-1, D.Holland 1-1, M.Lowe 3-3, Kirkman 2-2, Ja.Lopez 1-0. IBB-off M.Cain (Moreland). WP-M.Cain.

Umpires-Home, Sam Holbrook; First, Bill Miller; Second, Mike Winters; Third, Jeff Kellogg; Right, John Hirschbeck; Left, Gary Darling.

Time-3:17. Attendance-43,622 (41,815).

Above: Giants Pablo Sandoval. *Michael Macor | San Francisco Chronicle*

Upper Left: Center fielder Cody Ross rounds the bases on a solo homer. *Carlos Avila Gonzalez | San Francisco Chronicle*

Lower Left: Nate Schierholtz, Andres Torres and Manager Bruce Bochy down to their last out in the ninth inning. *Michael Macor | San Francisco Chronicle*

BOX SCORE

RANGERS 4, GIANTS 2

Giants	AB	R	H	BI	BB	SO	Avg.
A.Torres cf	4	1	1	1	0	0	.231
F.Sanchez 2b	4	0	1	0	0	0	.357
A.Huff 1b	3	0	1	0	0	0	.400
Posey c	3	0	1	0	1	1	.250
Burrell lf	4	0	0	0	0	4	.000
C.Ross rf	3	1	1	1	1	0	.300
Uribe 3b	4	0	0	0	0	1	.182
Sandoval dh	3	0	0	0	0	1	.000
Renteria ss	3	0	0	0	0	1	.300
Totals	31	2	5	2	2	8	

Rangers	AB	R	H	BI	BB	SO	Avg.
Andrus ss	4	0	2	0	0	1	.300
M.Young 3b	4	0	2	0	0	0	.250
J.Hamilton cf	4	1	1	1	0	0	.167
Guerrero dh	3	0	0	0	1	0	.143
N.Cruz lf	4	1	1	0	0	0	.154
Kinsler 2b	4	0	1	0	0	2	.250
Francoeur rf	2	0	0	0	1	1	.000
B.Molina c	1	1	0	0	2	0	.400
Moreland 1b	3	1	1	3	0	0	.500
Totals	29	4	8	4	4	4	

LINESCORE

Giants	000	000	110	-	2	5	1
Rangers	030	010	00x	-	4	8	0

E-Renteria (1). LOB-Giants 5, Texas 5. 2B-A.Huff (2), N.Cruz (2). HR-C.Ross (1), off C.Lewis; A.Torres (1), off C.Lewis; Moreland (1), off J.Sanchez; J.Hamilton (1), off J.Sanchez. RBIs-A.Torres (2), C.Ross (2), J.Hamilton (1), Moreland 3 (3). SB-Kinsler (1). CS-Guerrero (1). Runners moved up-J.Hamilton, Kinsler. GIDP-Sandoval, M.Young 2, B.Molina. DP-Giants 3 (Uribe, F.Sanchez, A.Huff), (Renteria, F.Sanchez, A.Huff), (Uribe, F.Sanchez, A.Huff); Texas 1 (Kinsler, Andrus, Moreland).

Giants	IP	H	R	ER	BB	SO	NP	ERA
J.Sanchez L, 0-1	4-2/3	6	4	4	3	3	72	7.71
Mota	1-1/3	1	0	0	1	0	21	0.00
Affeldt	1-1/3	1	0	0	0	0	15	6.75
R.Ramirez	2/3	0	0	0	0	1	7	18.00

Rangers	IP	H	R	ER	BB	SO	NP	ERA
C.Lewis W, 1-0	7-2/3	5	2	2	2	6	103	2.35
O'Day H, 1	1/3	0	0	0	0	0	7	13.50
N.Feliz S, 1-1	1	0	0	0	0	2	13	0.00

Inherited runners-scored-Mota 1-0, O'Day 1-0. HBP-by C.Lewis (A.Huff).

Umpires-Home, Bill Miller; First, Mike Winters; Second, Jeff Kellogg; Third, Gary Darling; Right, Sam Holbrook; Left, John Hirschbeck.

Time-2:51   Attendance-52,419 (49,170).

Above: Brian Wilson celebrates after the Giants defeated the Rangers 4-0.
Carlos Avila Gonzalez | San Francisco Chronicle

Left: Freddy Sanchez tumbles to earth after making a leaping catch to snare a Jeff Francoeur liner. *Lance Iversen | San Francisco Chronicle*

BOX SCORE

GIANTS 4, RANGERS 0

Giants	AB	R	H	BI	BB	SO	Avg.
A.Torres cf	5	1	3	1	0	0	.333
F.Sanchez 2b	4	0	0	0	0	0	.278
A.Huff dh	4	1	1	2	0	1	.357
Posey c	4	1	1	1	0	1	.250
C.Ross lf	3	0	0	0	1	1	.231
Uribe 3b	4	0	0	0	0	0	.133
Ishikawa 1b	3	0	0	0	1	1	.250
Renteria ss	4	1	3	0	0	1	.429
Schierholtz rf	4	0	0	0	0	1	.200
Totals	35	4	8	4	2	6	

Rangers	AB	R	H	BI	BB	SO	Avg.
Andrus ss	3	0	0	0	1	0	.231
M.Young 3b	4	0	1	0	0	2	.250
J.Hamilton cf	4	0	0	0	0	1	.125
Guerrero dh	3	0	0	0	0	3	.100
N.Cruz lf	3	0	1	0	0	0	.188
Kinsler 2b	2	0	0	0	1	0	.214
Francoeur rf	3	0	0	0	0	0	.000
B.Molina c	3	0	0	0	0	0	.250
Moreland 1b	3	0	1	0	0	2	.455
Totals	28	0	3	0	2	8	

LINESCORE

Giants	002	000	110 -	4	8	1
Rangers	000	000	000 -	0	3	0

E-Uribe (1). LOB-Giants 6, Texas 3. 2B-A.Torres 2 (4). HR-A.Huff (1), off Tom.Hunter; Posey (1), off O'Day. RBIs-A.Torres (3), A.Huff 2 (4), Posey (2). SB-A.Torres (1). CS-J.Hamilton (1). Runners moved up-A.Huff. GIDP-Andrus, J.Hamilton. DP-Giants 2 (F.Sanchez, Renteria, Ishikawa), (F.Sanchez, Renteria, Ishikawa).

Giants	IP	H	R	ER	BB	SO	NP	ERA
Bumgarner W, 1-0	8	3	0	0	2	6	106	0.00
Br.Wilson	1	0	0	0	0	2	11	0.00

Rangers	IP	H	R	ER	BB	SO	NP	ERA
Tom.Hunter L, 0-1	4	5	2	2	1	1	83	4.50
Ogando	1-2/3	0	0	0	0	2	19	0.00
D.Oliver	1-2/3	2	1	1	0	2	20	3.38
O'Day	2/3	1	1	1	0	1	19	13.50
D.Holland	1	0	0	0	1	1	20	27.00

Umpires-Home, Mike Winters; First, Jeff Kellogg; Second, Gary Darling; Third, John Hirschbeck; Right, Bill Miller; Left, Sam Holbrook.

Time-3:09   Attendance-51,920 (49,170).

Above: The Giants rushed the field after winning the final game of the World Series.
Carlos Avila Gonzalez | San Francisco Chronicle

Right: Brian Wilson and Tim Lincecum celebrate as the San Francisco Giants take game 5 to win the 2010 World Series.
Michael Macor | San Francisco Chronicle

Left: Tim Lincecum was nearly invincible on the mound and also light on his feet as he fielded this fifth-inning Bengie Molina grounder.
Carlos Avila Gonzalez | San Francisco Chronicle

Upper Left: Cody Ross, left, and Juan Uribe, far right, greet Edgar Renteria as he crosses the plate after hitting a three-run home run.
Lance Iversen | San Francisco Chronicle

BOX SCORE

GIANTS 3, RANGERS 1

Giants	AB	R	H	BI	BB	SO	Avg.
A.Torres rf	4	0	1	0	0	1	.318
F.Sanchez 2b	4	0	1	0	0	0	.273
Posey c	4	0	2	0	0	0	.300
C.Ross lf	4	1	1	0	0	1	.235
Uribe 3b	4	1	1	0	0	2	.158
A.Huff 1b	3	0	0	0	0	0	.294
Burrell dh	4	0	0	0	0	3	.000
Renteria ss	3	1	1	3	0	0	.412
Rowand cf	3	0	0	0	0	1	.250
Totals	33	3	7	3	0	8	

Rangers	AB	R	H	BI	BB	SO	Avg.
Andrus ss	4	0	0	0	0	1	.176
M.Young 3b	4	0	1	0	0	0	.250
J.Hamilton cf	4	0	0	0	0	2	.100
Guerrero dh	4	0	0	0	0	1	.071
N.Cruz rf	4	1	1	1	0	2	.200
Kinsler 2b	2	0	0	0	1	0	.188
Dav.Murphy lf	3	0	0	0	0	3	.143
B.Molina c	3	0	0	0	0	2	.182
Moreland 1b	2	0	1	0	1	1	.462
Totals	30	1	3	1	2	12	

LINESCORE

Giants	000	000	300	-	3	7	0		
Rangers	000	000	100	-	1	3	1		

E-Moreland (1). LOB-Giants 4, Texas 4. HR-Renteria (2), off Cl.Lee; N.Cruz (1), off Lincecum. RBIs-Renteria 3 (6), N.Cruz (3). S-A.Huff. GIDP-Renteria. DP-Texas 1 (Andrus, Kinsler, Moreland).

Giants	IP	H	R	ER	BB	SO	NP	ERA
Lincecum W, 2-0	8	3	1	1	2	10	101	3.29
Br.Wilson S, 1-1	1	0	0	0	0	2	11	0.00

Rangers	IP	H	R	ER	BB	SO	NP	ERA
Cl.Lee L, 0-2	7	6	3	3	0	6	95	6.94
N.Feliz	2	1	0	0	0	2	23	0.00

Umpires-Home, Jeff Kellogg; First, Gary Darling; Second, John Hirschbeck; Third, Sam Holbrook; Right, Mike Winters; Left, Bill Miller.

Time-2:32   Attendance-52,045 (49,170).

San Francisco Giants' players wave to the crowd at the end of the ceremony at Civic Center Plaza. *Lea Suzuki | San Francisco Chronicle*

CHAMPIONSHIP DRAWS ALL KINDS OF GIANTS, FANS TOGETHER TO CELEBRATE

BY GWEN KNAPP

Has any other World Series parade yielded references to the Grateful Dead and the Beatles, mention of a ballot measure to legalize recreational marijuana, allusions to an S&M character, and the sight of the first baseman shoving a hand down his pants to extract a piece of lingerie?

After making San Francisco history on Monday night by winning the city's first World Series trophy, the Giants staged a uniquely stylish celebration on Wednesday. As the players came together at the City Hall stage, they made quite a picture, some of them reflecting the extreme quirks of their baseball home, others bringing a more straightforward, earnest quality to the proceedings.

During the speeches, the immaculately groomed Buster Posey sat next to shaggy-haired Tim Lincecum, and not far from Brian Wilson's Mohawk and iconic beard. Second baseman Freddy Sanchez thanked God. Center fielder Andres Torres saluted his wife's birthday. First baseman Aubrey Huff waved his famed thong at the crowd.

Yet, somehow, they harmonized beautifully, just as they had on the field over the last past month, when they took down Atlanta, Philadelphia and Texas to bring home the gleaming trophy that manager Bruce Bochy carried throughout the parade.

The outrageous humor of Huff and Wilson will be embedded forever in the memories of Giants fans, but so will the succinct staunchness of Posey. In a forceful voice that belied his rookie status, the catcher told everyone to enjoy the title for about a week. "Then let's get back to work, and make another run at it," he said, pounding the podium as he stepped away.

The parade itself borrowed some vintage touches, using replica motorized cable cars favored by the 49ers in their Super Bowl era and following the route taken by the 1958 Giants on their introductory ride.

Most of the players wore fashion-forward T-shirts, which paid homage to both the World Series and the intricate patterns of tattoo art. But back-up catcher Eli Whiteside proudly wore the iconic Deadhead version of a Giants T-shirt, and reliever Sergio Romo chose a Beatles motif.

Centerfielder Andres Torres arrived at City Hall in a short leather jacket over a white T-shirt. But when he went to his seat, teammates chided him, practically stripping the jacket off his back. Laughing, he took an orange T-shirt from the supply the players would later toss to the crowd and quickly pulled it over his head.

Huff, not surprisingly, seemed to be leading the charge to disrobe Torres. He had turned a red thong into one of the many odd symbols of the Giants' championship run, following in the path of another Bay Area first baseman, Jason Giambi, who pioneered the thong-as-talisman concept with a gold model.

Above: Fans throng San Francisco's Market Street to watch the Giants' World Series parade. *Kirsten Aguilar* | *San Francisco Chronicle*

At different points of the parade route, Huff could be seen wearing the famed Rally Thong over his jeans and twirling or waving it at fans. But at the City Hall finish line, Huff waited until his turn at the microphone to bring the thong out of hiding and send the throng at Civic Center Plaza into a frenzy. After thanking the Giants for signing him last off-season, Huff plunged his hand under his waistband and rooted around forever. If he fielded that slowly and awkwardly, he'd never have made the majors.

Producing the slip of red fabric, he shouted: "The rally thong is going to the Hall of Fame. Or maybe we'll just wear it next spring training."

Wilson ended his raucous speech by asking: "Where's the Machine?" a cryptic comment to anyone who had not seen footage of the closer's nationally televised interview from home, where a man dressed in a leather mask and little else strolls through the background.

Any suspicion that Wilson might dial back his big personality vanished when he informed the crowd that he thought he was having a small heart attack. "I'm not sure what it's from," he said. "Maybe the electricity in the crowd, or maybe the smell of Prop. 19."

The ballot measure to legalize marijuana failed at the polls Tuesday, but a distinctly herbal aroma, ever-present near the ballpark's McCovey Cove this postseason, still pervaded the plaza.

Lincecum avoided the issue, even though his off-season misdemeanor for pot possession launched a thousand "Let Timmy Smoke" shirts. He kept his remarks simple and G-rated, without a hint of the publicly uttered "F- Yeah" that colored his response to winning the division and launched another thousand T-shirts.

In many ways, he couldn't be more different from? Posey, whose idea of an imprecation is "Oh, darn." But as they sat side by side on Wednesday, they constantly talked to each other and broke into simultaneous grins, acting like inseparable friends who have something very fundamental in common. They do. It begins again in February, when pitchers and catchers report to Arizona.■

Giants mascot Lou Seal makes an confetti angel along Montgomery Street, as San Francisco celebrates the World Series Champion Giants.

Michael Macor | San Francisco Chronicle